JOURNEY
with
the POOR

JOURNEY
with
the POOR

PETER PHILP

Collins Dove

Published by COLLINS DOVE
60-64 Railway Road, Blackburn, Victoria 3130
Telephone (03) 877 1333

Cover Designed by Joanne Brazil
Typeset in 11 on 12½ Cheltenham Book by Bookset, Vic.
Cover photograph and photographs throughout the book by Peter Philp
Printed in Australia by Globe Press, Vic.
Reprinted 1988

The National Library of Australia
Cataloguing-in-Publication data:

Philp, Peter, 1943-
    Journey with the poor.

    ISBN 0 85924 562 4.

    1. Church and the poor – Developing countries.
    2. Social justice. 3. Church and the world.
    I. Title.

261.8

CONTENTS

Dedicated to the powerless ones
in Latin America, particularly
in El Salvador, who have inspired
me so much.

FOREWORD

Latin America is a melting pot of need, inequality, power struggles, rich cultural traditions, militarisation, human rights abuses, democratic and authoritarian movements, and diverse theological streams. Within this complex and difficult context, the church and Christian agencies like World Vision struggle to forge a meaningful role in Latin American society. Over the past few decades Australians have begun to recognise that we are closely linked to Asia. Media coverage of recent major disasters in Africa has also focused public attention on this needy continent. Meanwhile, Latin America has largely remained a shadowy region, little understood by Australians despite the contribution that Latin American migrants have made to the multicultural fabric of Australian society.

World Vision began working in Latin America in the 1960s, with a major expansion of our program in the mid-1970s. Today there are World Vision projects in more than 20 countries of Central and South America and the island nations of the Caribbean. World Vision's programs in Latin America concentrate mainly on rural community development, urban slum programs and emergency relief.

World Vision has had a long history of providing relief assistance in times of disaster. Examples have included the 1976 earthquake in Guatemala, floods in Ecuador (1982), drought in Bolivia and Peru (1983), the volcanic eruption in Colombia in 1986; and assistance over several years to Central American refugees.

Community development programs seek to assist local communities to become self-reliant through a variety of agricultural, economic, environmental, health and education programs. In Haiti there has been a strong emphasis on replanting the denuded and eroded hillsides. In Guatemala collective farm school programs train local villagers in animal husbandry, crop diversification, elementary education and basic literacy. World Vision Peru has particularly assisted deprived indigenous Indian communities in agriculture, health, literacy, nutrition, income-generation projects and Christian leadership.

Latin America's burgeoning cities receive a continuous stream of the rural poor. World Vision's urban programs seek to help families struggling valiantly to build a future for themselves and their children in the urban slums. Some aspects of these programs are improved housing, education, water supplies, sanitation, nutritional feeding, health education, and community groups meeting to solve local problems together.

Our work in Latin America has not been easy. The issues which confront us of injustice, inequality, exploitation and violence, make working with the poor challenging and sometimes dangerous. Project workers and staff have faced threats to their safety. As an organization we have faced many challenges in our Christian pilgrimage on this continent. We in World Vision of Australia share in partnership with our Latin American field staff in their hopes, struggles and ministry.

Peter Philp has played a particularly meaningful role in this partnership. His visits to Latin America have always provided a rich input of information and challenge to World Vision staff and supporters and the wider Australian community.

Peter's words do not always leave us comfortable. He has sought to let those he has met tell their stories of pain, struggle and hope; with the aim that we may take up God's call to seek justice, love, mercy and walk humbly with our God.

Harold Henderson
Executive Director
World Vision of Australia

UN OBISPO MORIRA PERO LA IGLESIA DE DIOS QUE ES EL PUEBLO NO PERECERA JAMAS**

Mons. Romero

Oscar Romero understood that he was going to die violently. However, he knew that resurrection always followed death. The Archbishop said: 'A bishop will die, but the church of God, which is the people, will never perish.'

INTRODUCTION

My journey with the poor has been long, and at times somewhat simplistic and confused.

From my earliest recollections the plight of the poor was emphasised at home and school. I remember as a youngster collecting and selling beer bottles to help the work of the missionaries. Most of my reading about the poor in those days was restricted to the *Far East*, the missionary magazine of the Columban Fathers. I suspect that my motivation for reading the publication had more to do with a column called Mickey Daley's Diary than the lives of the underprivileged.

The poor were a blur. They were people in Africa, India and China living in broken-down houses with little to eat. However, I was aware of poverty very close to home — in a park situated a few streets from the family house.

Here was a collection of homeless drunks, taking cover in the long grass and in a few disused drain pipes. And when the rains came, they would leave the park and move to a nearby tram shelter-shed until the police picked them up.

The sight of these poor left a deep impression on me. It was one of fear. I used to have nightmares about them. I still have vivid memories of the middle-aged women in filthy clothes, stockings draped around their ankles and blood smeared over their cut legs and faces. I would wake up during some winter nights, believing that they were trying to force their way into our house.

But I always saw a natural connection between the church and the poor. There was Damien who gave up his life for the lepers on Molokai and Francis of Assisi who went out to serve the poor. These people seemed to me to be examples of what Christianity was all about.

As a broadcaster and journalist, I gradually developed a deeper interest in the poor. They were much less of a blur. This was the 1960s, when media people were taking less and less interest in archbishops' statements and considered that much of what the church was doing and saying was irrelevant to the issues of the day.

The media focused attention on those whom it considered the real reformers. Reporters were going out to cover student protests. These were colourful and controversial, and the media saw the students as representing people with idealistic dreams, young people who were demanding change in their society.

The media were always prepared to feature people like Mother Teresa and Martin Luther King. My colleagues and I had similar expectations to mine in regard to the church. They saw that direct connection between the church and the people of poverty.

During a period of my working career in Sale, Victoria, I drew closer to God, trying to hear his message to me.

In 1976, I joined World Vision and so began a new phase in my journey. My life became centred around the poor. Yet this was a time of confusion in many ways. For the first time in my life, I began to ask questions about the poor and the causes of their poverty. I discovered that it was in the interests of a minority to keep two thirds of the world in poverty. I began to understand words like power, oppression, justice and responsibility. I quickly learned four things.

First, to be effective in this ministry I had to know the poor. To work for a Christian humanitarian aid agency doesn't guarantee one's understanding of the poor. Similarly, not all members of the church have a deep understanding of God and the demands made by a commitment to his work.

Second, I came to understand that involvement with the poor is a responsibility and not a good turn.

Third, that everyone has a unique role to play. It isn't merely the giving of money that reforms, it is commitment to changing self and structures.

Fourth, it is essential to know the mind of Christ. He has a lot more to say about the relations between the rich and the poor than many Christians are prepared to admit.

Most of my journey thus far had concentrated on the poor in Africa and Asia.

In 1980, World Vision's executive director, Harold Henderson, sent me to Latin America. That experience changed my direction completely. Here I confronted the poor. Here I saw a new and dynamic dimension of Christianity.

One hot Sunday afternoon in the Mexican slums, I sat with a disciple who further shattered so much of the old, and took my journey to the front line of the action. Alberto Navarro is a Jesuit priest. He spoke about the new conversion that the church was experiencing, and how bishops, priests and nuns were learning anew from the poor. He spoke about empowering the poor and putting aside things in our Christian tradition for which we might hold fond memories, but which were a means of power to oppress. Alberto said to me that after his conversion to the poor Archbishop Romero had begun reading the Bible 'from a different place'.

To understand God and His poor, maybe we all need to read the Word from a different place. Though much of what Alberto Navarro had to say seemed threatening to me at the time, he prepared me for my journey into the lives of persecuted El Salvadorans and Guatemalans. Alberto will always be a very special friend.

Most of us in the West see ourselves, in relation to the poor, as the providers, directors and good samaritans. This mindset results in the poor remaining the receivers, listeners, obligators — the oppressed.

We all have opportunities to travel with the poor. I thank God that so many have been given to me. I thank Harold Henderson for the trust that he continues to place in me, and those Christian partners whose directions were not always the same as mine. We all need guidance and theirs was invaluable.

Most of all I want to thank the poor. They have taught me so much — to be a receiver, a listener and a partner.

Peter Philp

One of the greatest sins of violence and oppression is the deep scars left on the children. Man's inhumanity to man always abuses the children

CHAPTER I

MEDELLIN

A Voice Cries in the Wilderness

Suddenly nobody was laughing. Stories about banana republics and infamous dictators, who ran their countries like a three-ring circus, no longer seemed funny.

The despatches from Central America were sombre. They talked about death squads and terrorised people. They reported the assassination of priests and Protestant pastors. They shocked the world with the news that an archbishop had been murdered at the Eucharistic table while celebrating Mass.

Neither poverty nor brutal oppression is a startling new phenomenon in Latin America. The poor have lived under grinding repression, first during the time of the Spanish Conquistadors and then under land-owning oligarchies which formed soon after independence.

However, the 1970s ushered some significant new elements into this neo-feudal existence. An awareness began to emerge in peasant communities. The church began to convince the poor that they were important in the sight of God; that they had basic human rights to education, free speech, equitable wages; and a role in the electoral process of their country. Popular peoples' movements also evolved, which emphasised change through active political involvement, and if that failed mobilisation for an armed struggle.

By and large, the church up to that time had not been an

active voice for human rights. Traditionally, the Catholic Church had identified with the ruling elite.

Vatican II and the historic Latin American Bishops' Conference at Medellin, Colombia in 1968, started to change the face of the church. It was as though God had seized his church and shaken new life and awareness into it. To be faithful to the Gospel, the church had to confront the issues of the wretched poverty and injustice surrounding it. The Medellin documents spoke about 'a preferential option for the poor'. But to involve oneself with the outcasts of Latin society meant to confront the rich and powerful. The oligarchies, the military, the multinational companies and conservative sections of the Christian Church, saw this as a betrayal — as a church that had gone crazy; a church swinging dangerously to the left.

Many bishops who had agreed in principle to the preferential option for the poor at Medellin decided that they were not yet prepared to turn their face to Jerusalem and walk to Calvary.

But for others there was no turning back. Cardinals, bishops, priests and lay people abandoned privilege and security to assume the role of servant-hood and persecution.

The warnings came, but God's disciples stood by their commitment to the poor. Priests and nuns were accused of being subversives. When the spreading of scandal did not work, physical violence was introduced. Some clergy were arrested and tortured.

In San Salvador slogans were painted on the city walls: 'Be a patriot and kill a priest'.

And they did. The first was a champion of the poor, a Jesuit, Rutilio Grande. His assassination led his archbishop, Oscar Romero, to an extraordinary conversion.

Before Grande's death, Romero had been a conservative and cautious man. Three years later, Romero too died at the hands of a terror squad.

Another major change occurred in the 1970s. The world started to discover the reality of this distant and somewhat mysterious region. It began not only to understand the difference between South America and Central America, but that these small Central American states had names like Nicaragua, Guatemala and El Salvador.

However, the media's sudden interest in this forgotten and shamefully exploited section of our planet was not motivated by humanitarian feelings. There was a revolution brewing in Nicaragua and sinister bloodletting in neighbouring El Salvador. This was good for reader circulation and viewer ratings.

I too had been guilty of laughing at the corruption and abuse of power in Latin America.

However, it was not the sensational headlines of the international press that brought home to me the richness of these people, but the writings of Archbishop Dom Helder Camara. The words of this tiny Brazilian prophet forced me to read more. Listen to the poor and work with them, he would say. He did not shirk dealing with gross injustices, despite state persecution of his priests. But he was not a prophet of doom. Hope was Camara's message. The words that had the greatest impact on me were: 'When shall we have the courage to outgrow the charity mentality and see that at the bottom of all relations between rich and poor there is a problem of justice?'.

Even though I did not realise it at the time, my interest in Latin America was the beginning of a process that had reached into the hearts of cardinals, priests, Protestant pastors and the poor themselves. I was discovering Christ. I was undergoing a conversion.

I was tuning into the live sounds of the exciting Central American church. Via tense telephone conversations, I was slipping into a close union with these suffering people. The written word was inspiring, but listening to frontline disciples who spoke to me personally about what it was like to be a Christian in El Salvador was vastly more enriching.

'Life in El Salvador is horrible. The life of every priest in our country is being threatened by those who have no respect for human beings. This year an archbishop, ten priests, three nuns and a lay missionary have been assassinated and two other priests have disappeared, believed killed,' exclaimed one senior church official.

At the height of this crazy killing, when to proclaim the liber-

3

ating Gospel of Jesus Christ was more inflammatory than reading Karl Marx, I listened to a priest in San Salvador expressing his fears, his faith and his hope to me over the telephone. His courage astonished me. Each word of the telephone conversation was being carefully monitored and the very act of speaking the truth could bring bloody repercussions. The forces of evil had done it before to Father Grande and to Archbishop Romero.

He had been a close associate of Oscar Romero. There was no doubt his phone was tapped. I asked him questions. Boldly he responded. I was asking him to put his life on the line so that I could gain information. He had agreed. Suddenly I realised that this information placed a grave responsibility on me.

I was not a doctor to go and bind up the bleeding bodies of his parishioners. I was not a person of great influence who could be heard in the corridors of power. I was not a priest who could go and replace those members of his pastoral team who had been struck down.

It seemed as though I was not much help to him in his hour of greatest need. Yet I was exposing him to death by asking him to speak.

In the liberation of God's poor and oppressed, every man, woman and child has a role to play. I asked the priest what I could do — what the Australian people could do.

He quickly replied. 'The church of El Salvador calls on all Catholics and Protestants to pray and to be concerned for our people.

'Pray for my country.

'Let the truth of El Salvador be known to all your people.

'Write to the junta in El Salvador and ask it to stop killing.

'Write to the Australian Government so that it can use its influence with the junta.

'And help our people with material aid.'

He did not have the access to the media or the opportunity that I had. I was a journalist and a broadcaster. I had the freedom of speech. In the security of Australia I could do some-

4

thing that he could not; tell Australians the truth so they could mobilise in prayer, and protest about the slaughter of the Salvadoran people.

Put your ear to the ground
and listen,
hurried, worried footsteps, bitterness, rebellion.
Listen again.
Put out feelers.
The Lord is there.
— **Dom Helder Camara**

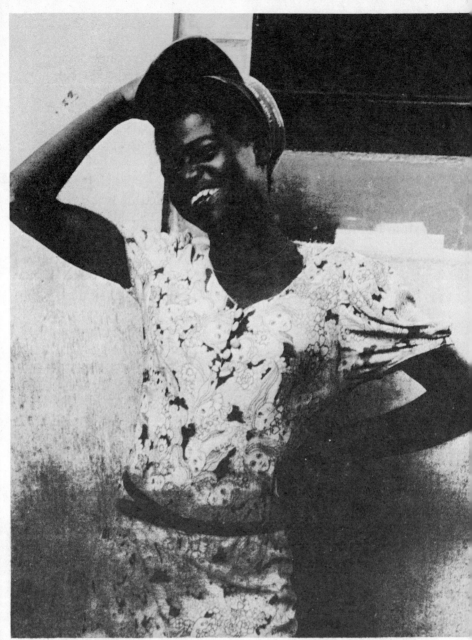

Isobelle, a change agent in her community. Real reform will not occur in the Third World unless it is initiated by the poor themselves.

CHAPTER II

BRAZIL

The Beginning

El Salvador was my confirmation. Through this remarkable experience I gained new vision, real commitment and witnessed courageous faith in Christ.

But before confirmation there was baptism, my initiation into God's extended family, the people who comprise two-thirds of our world — the poor. My pilgrimage had its genesis in the largest Christian nation on earth, Brazil.

Up until this time, my perception of poverty and its root causes was superficial.

For many years I had a deep interest in the social dimensions of the Gospel. I always had an affinity with the outcasts, therefore was ready to support the causes of charity and compassion. My concern for the underprivileged led me from a long career in broadcasting to the nerve centre of an international aid agency.

Despite all that, I was basically ignorant of the poor. Maybe it was my conservative Irish-Catholic upbringing. But then not all my ancestors could be considered conservative. Queen Victoria of Great Britain had jailed a great-great-grand uncle for subversion in Ireland in the 1800s and the same British monarch had placed a price on the head of another relative for leading Australia's only armed rebellion.

While proud of our great-great-grandfathers' exploits in Australia, nevertheless time and circumstances gradually rendered later generations more conservative and cautious. I was very much a product of these later generations.

In Brazil it was a series of events, none in themselves dramatic, that thrust me into deep and sometimes dangerous waters. Every time I tried to pull myself free from these troubled waters, some person or experience pushed me further into these uncertain places.

My entry into Brazil was through the isolated city of Manaus, in the vast empty north. Travelling around Manaus I had been captivated by the majestic churches, its florid market and its river — the mighty Amazon.

Take a boat out into the middle of this massive waterway and see where the feeder rivers, the Rio Negro and the Rio Silomos, rush in swirling their individual colours into the Amazon. You can clearly see the dark blackish water from the Negro and the yellow water of the Silomos rush together before being swallowed up by the enormous flowing currents of the Amazon.

Surprisingly it was not the Amazon that left the greatest impression on me during my stopover in Manaus, but an appendage that clung precariously to the muddy edge of the mighty river.

For a long time, I stood and gazed from a high embankment down onto a cluster of iron and timber shanties. No longer was I reading books or watching films. There, within a few yards of me, was graphic Third World poverty.

My reaction? Anger. 'My God how can this happen? How can it happen in a Christian country?'

Standing on that embankment and gazing down on this abysmal squalor, all of Manaus' splendour disappeared. I was flooded by an ocean of pity for the people and by a torrent of guilt for my inadequacy to do anything dramatic to cure what I saw.

This was a sudden realisation that I had stepped out onto a precipice and there displayed before me was the exposed soul of my ministry.

I was shattered that life could be as depressed as this. And yet, all I had seen was a collection of shanties. I was yet to experience the broken and scarred lives that attempted to exist under these shelters. This Australian humanitarian was raw, but very soon he would sit and listen to the words of very special teachers.

From Manaus, we flew the milk run down the Atlantic coast, eventually planning to land in the Brazilian city of Salvador. Here I was to spend a day meeting development and church leaders. The jet pulled to a halt, the third or was it the fourth time that morning. I had lost count. I tried to remember by recalling how many snacks I had had on the flight. Light refreshments were served on each leg of the trip.

My head was whirling and aching. The flight had left Manaus about 3am and we had done nothing but land and take off. It was St Patrick's Day and I was trying to compose a letter to my family in Australia.

The flight steward approached and paused. I was waiting for her to ask 'Tea or coffee, sir?'. But this time she enquired: 'Are you Mr Philp from World Vision?'.

'Yes', I replied.

'Your office has requested that you disembark here instead of Salvador.'

I did not argue; fresh air and my feet firmly on the ground again was all I wanted. In the rush to pick up my baggage, I forgot to ask the crew just where we were.

Crossing the tarmac I glanced up at the terminal building to find a name.

'Well look where we are', I called to my companion. 'Recife.'

'Yes', he replied. 'I am not sure just where it is in relation to Salvador.'

I was not sure either, but the place was very familiar to me.

'You know who lives here, don't you?' I asked. 'Dom Helder Camara.'

'Does he? We should try to call around to see him', said my colleague.

And try we did. I was aware that the government, military and police were threatened by this archbishop, but I did not expect this fear to extend to Christian friends.

Our hosts in Recife were very disturbed by the idea of my meeting with the archbishop. One friend said that Camara was ill in bed and could not see anyone. Later, I was told that he was in Europe. Even the idea of calling at his office to meet his staff caused consternation.

The opposition to going anywhere near Helder Camara's office, home or church continued. Some Christians explained that if they were seen near the archbishop or his staff, they too might be accused by the authorities of being leftist sympathisers.

The next morning I had breakfast with a Baptist minister who pastored the largest Baptist community in that city. He was tipped to be appointed the next director of World Vision of Brazil.

Rev Manfred Grellert spoke openly about the injustice in his country and the need for Christians to get out and get dirty with the poor. My interest in Dom Helder was raised. Grellert mentioned that he was a good friend of the archbishop's.

'Would you like to meet him?' enquired Grellert.

'But I've been told he is sick or in Europe,' I replied.

'Dom Helder is okay. He is leading a bishops' meeting in the neighbouring city of Olinda. We could go to his early morning Mass or to the conference centre.'

The old city of Olinda has not changed since its colonial days. The churches are grander than those of Manaus, and the narrow cobblestoned streets snake up steep hills and disappear suddenly around sharp curves. The tiny stone houses on either side of the streets are superbly preserved.

On the way to the conference centre we passed the old weather-beaten white church where Dom Helder Camara lived and celebrated his morning Mass. On the side of the building was an old wooden door where he appeared each morning to talk with the poor who congregated to meet their archbishop. He never let anybody go away hungry.

As I sat in the spacious entry hall of the Jesuit centre, I wondered what the man whom I was about to meet would be like. The man whose proclamation of the Gospel terrified the Brazilian authorities as much as it apparently threatened the Jewish leaders 2000 years ago. The man who had been banned from the media, because his message was contrary to the doctrine of National Security practised by the rightist military dictatorship in Brazil. Dom Helder Camara, the man regarded by the military and the police as the subversive or, as he was commonly known, the Red Archbishop, but the same man that nobody dared touch. Instead the authorities arrested and tortured his friends. And I wondered about an archbishop who was prepared to interrupt a conference to meet an Australian whom he had never heard of — and at five minutes' notice. I was sure such a man would find plenty of time to stop and share with his poor.

Then he appeared. A tiny person, dwarfed by the large stone pillars, stooped and looking very tired and fragile. Dom Helder was dressed in his cream cassock with a small brown wooden cross. The most vivid memory I have of him, as he walked across the entry hall, is his huge smile and his outstretched hands.

'Welcome my brother from Australia.' Certainly not the introduction you expect from an archbishop suddenly disturbed during a major conference.

We spoke briefly together then he suggested that I rejoin him at his office later in the day.

What was once the palatial home of the archbishops of Recife and Olinda, where the rich and powerful were entertained by past monsignors, today serves as a medical centre, advice bureau and legal aid office for the people of Recife.

We sat together and Dom Helder spoke about many things. His concern was for the subhuman conditions in which his people lived, not only here in the north-east, but throughout Brazil, and in all parts of Latin America. He spoke about the exploitative action of multi-national corporations, which held both worker and country to ransom, threatening to set up operations elsewhere unless very favourable conditions were given to them.

He spoke about the repression of the people by military dictators who protected their power by instigating the doctrine of National Security, which allowed individual rights to be grossly abused so that the law and order of the nation could be maintained.

11

However the archbishop was not a prophet of doom. He predicted great hope. The laws within Brazil were liberalising. He reminded me too that our hope lies in Christ with the knowledge that He is always with us.

'Real change,' said Dom Helder, 'will not come with violence and armaments. It will come through our Creator who loves His people. We must believe in Him.'

On another occasion I met him at the Brazilian Bishops' Conference at the old Jesuit retreat house at Itaici, near Sao Paulo. He was the same quiet gentle person, ready to give his time, despite his heavy schedule. He again impressed on me the importance of understanding the root causes of poverty. If we could own up to our responsibilities then charity and international aid would not be an ongoing demand, he reminded me.

And most of all he gave me encouragement to continue to push out into the desert of poverty, knowing that the trek would be overpowering at times, but it would not be in vain. Oh how I needed those words. Doing the job that I do, that desert often looks so formidable.

That same day I spent a few moments with another fearless Christian, Dom Paulo Arns, the Cardinal Archbishop of Sao Paulo, a man who had chosen servanthood instead of princedom. Down in the sprawling slums of Sao Paulo his role of servant had developed him into a dynamic leader of the people, which could never have occurred if he had merely elected to assume his official duties as Prince of the Church.

At our meeting, Dom Paulo emphasised to me the necessity for unity, whether it be the poor in their communities, the bishops in their conference, or the bishops in the community with the poor.

'People are coming together, the poor. They assemble and find new strength,' said the cardinal.

Already these people have seen change occur. In one area thousands formed a delegation to request a clean water supply. When this huge number turned up on the mayor's doorstep he was unable to refuse. Workers in Sao Paulo have mobilised together and gained better wage justice.

Rather than speak about what the church has done for the poor, he prefers to speak about what the poor have done for the church and each other.

'They (the poor) will show us a third way — not totalitarian socialism, nor what I call savage capitalism. The poor will find their liberation in the light of the Gospel which they reflect on and believe in.'

He suggested that the people of Nicaragua were attempting to move towards a third way, and hoped that while this Central American republic wrestles its way through the difficult times of transition, the church will not reject this nation.

To be with these prophets is one experience, to walk through a crumbling Brazilian *favela* is another. Masses of tiny shanties, huddled together on the sides of steep hills and valleys. Straw, rotting timber and rusted iron sheets provide minimal protection for hundreds of families. The narrow alleyways that separate these houses are open sewers, which rise and flood through the shacks in the wet season, and in dry conditions become a multitude of fly-infested deep furrows.

People merely exist, rather than live, in these conditions. Crime is rampant. The poor become prey to the drug and vice mafia who spread their greedy tentacles around these vulnerable victims. The police raid the communities to hunt out bottom-level criminals or simply to torment the helpless poor who are defenceless to fight back.

Inside these wretched places a remarkable phenomenon is under way that has had a radical effect on Latin America's political and church life — the Base Christian Community.

New and vibrant life is bursting out of these surroundings that have known only violence and destitution. The Catholic Church and some other Christian and humanitarian groups have been catalysts in this amazing revolution. However, the roots of the change are the poor themselves.

They are finding new awareness, pride and belief in themselves and an uncomplicated understanding of the relationship between life and God.

I had spent most of the day tracking through some *favelas* on the outskirts of Belo Horizonte with some World Vision project workers. We had spoken to a number of smiling people who were participating in the projects.

The last call for the day was on a women's sewing and hygiene centre at the rear of a Protestant church. There I noticed a girl standing by the church door. She was black and there was something about this young woman that attracted my attention.

'She comes very often to help us,' mentioned one of the project staff. 'She assists in setting up sewing classes. She is a very caring person.'

The girl smiled and I walked over to her and through my interpreter, struck up a conversation.

The most interesting part of my day was about to commence.

Isabelle was 14. She was completing her sixth grade studies at the local school, and was determined to reach grade eight level.

After a little talking, we became friends. She was keen to show me around her village. I sensed straight away that she was proud of her community. Eager to learn more, I accepted her invitation.

'I want to be a secretary,' she told me as we began to walk down one of the laneways between the box-like shanties.

'I think I could do the job well. When I am a secretary, I would like to meet a handsome young man and get married.'

Fifteen minutes ago she was the girl standing by the church door, a total stranger. Despite our language barriers we were now like a couple of children, laughing, stopping at a small stall to buy icecream, and asking each other silly questions.

She continually stopped to show me things and introduce me to people. All of this was a new adventure. Yet I had been trudging through *favelas* all day. The difference now was that one of the community had invited me to join her on a visit. Earlier I had been part of an official party from an international aid agency. The community was now accepting me as somebody they had brought into their village. Those we spoke to were at ease. I was not there for an official inspection.

'This is Patricia my friend. She lives in that stone house,' called Isabelle.

Patricia joined us for a short time. When we reached her gate, Patricia invited us to see her dolls.

The next moment I was walking into a crowded little room, being introduced to a party of smiling brown faces. Nobody, I'm sure, was quite certain who I was, but they accepted me as a friend of Isabelle. I was led into the bedroom, a neat and very clean room. A number of dolls were arranged on the bed.

Just like young teenagers in Australia, both girls began to giggle as they told me the names of the dolls.

Back on the street, we stopped and spoke with a middle-aged man who was laying some bricks.

'You are from Australia,' he replied in very broken English. 'I have been to your country. The place, I think they call it Sydney.'

He was a retired police officer, who had spent time in Australia serving at the Brazilian Embassy.

'Come inside and see what I am building,' he said. He was helping to construct a small cafe.

My chance meeting with Isabelle gave me a rare opportunity to become part of the community for a short time. I too was amazed at the way young Isabelle was handling the situation. Being black she belonged to the bottom rung of the *favela* ladder. The darker your skin the lower your status. Yet this girl was the VIP, like the mayor, showing around an overseas guest.

The girl excitedly chatted about her home and how her mother would love to meet me.

I had noticed that the shanty town was deteriorating rapidly as we moved down into a valley.

There were no more brick or stone houses. Rotting timber and old corrugated iron humpies dotted both sides of the ravine. The area smelt of damp. The rutted paths were slippery with slime. Everything had changed, except Isabelle. At the base of the ravine, numerous rivulets of green and bluish water formed a drain. People walked through this bog and little children crawled and played nearby. This was their only alternative to being shut away in one of the shanties.

15

Isabelle stopped at the gate leading to a tiny mud and stick house, badly discoloured by years of heavy pollution.

Her broad smiling face was saying: 'Welcome to my home.'

And it was not merely a house, but a home. The four small smoky rooms accommodated a family of eleven. It was now well into the evening and the house was almost dark.

The girl's mother, Marguerita, stood at a stove preparing stew for the evening meal. Like her daughter she was happy to welcome me without any hint of embarrassment.

Isabelle's father was a carpenter. He brought home $150 a month. Most of this was swallowed up paying rent for the shanty.

Taking my hand Isabelle led me into a pocket-handkerchief backyard. A large face appeared from behind some packing cases and snorted at me. It was the family pig, a prized possession. Marguerita had managed to save and buy the animal. It cost her $15. In a few weeks the pig would be fattened and could be sold for $60 at the market. The mother planned to buy two more pigs with the proceeds and invest the remainder to provide some essential items for the family.

Marguerita was active in the community and was determined to provide for her children and not depend on continuous charity.

Isabelle walked me back to my car. Maybe she would never be a secretary in Belo Horizonte. And somehow I hoped she would not take it on. If she did the community would lose her.

In our short time together, Isabelle had demonstrated her leadership qualities. The community needed people like her if they were to rise above this poverty.

'Here is your World Vision project manager of tomorrow, or your social worker,' I said as we climbed into the car.

Change must come in these impoverished *favelas*. And if that change is to be effective, the Dom Helders, Dom Paulos and World Visions can only be catalysts, the Isabelles will be the real architects and builders.

I came to understand the message of the prophets and the message of Jesus; but the God who revealed himself to us in the Bible isn't a neutral God, but a God who takes sides with the poor. And therefore we, as priest-prophets of the church of the New Testament, can't be neutral either.

Before I left their shanty town in Medellin, I swore to them I'd devote my life, all the life left to me, to fighting for the liberation of the poor.

— **Fernando Cardinal SJ, Nicaragua**

Violence is common in Latin America. In most of the conflict it is the civilians who die or are crippled, and not the soldiers or guerillas.

CHAPTER III

The Song of the Hillside Servant

Colombians will tell you that their country is the cultural centre of Latin America.

There is no doubt that Colombia has inherited a deep and rich tradition in the arts, particularly in its music, that is difficult to equal in the Americas.

The capital, Bogota, too, can boast about its exceptional beauty. Its grand churches, civic buildings and commercial district have retained a unique charm that many Latin cities have lost under years of neglect, smog and civil strife.

To stroll through Bogota at dawn is an experience to be treasured.

The city is already alive with movement. The lines of donkeys wait, tied to railings while their masters collect the scraps from the city's restaurants. Priests, dressed in their black cassocks, hurry down cobble-stoned alleys on their way to early morning Mass. People sit with the flocks of birds in the square waiting for the massive wooden doors of the cathedral to grind open. A weird and wonderful collection of 'Yank tanks', many of them museum pieces from the motoring forties and fifties, rumble through the streets polluting the morning air with their exhaust fumes.

In central Bogota, everything seems equal at that time of day. There are no immediate scenes of gruelling poverty. These are certainly present, but for now are hidden away with the other realities of life in Colombia.

At dawn, one is afforded the rare opportunity to stroll idly along these footpaths. The heavy aggressive Colombian pedestrian traffic has yet to emerge. But even so early, it is not wise to walk these streets alone, especially with an expensive camera slung around your neck.

What Colombians do not boast about is their horrific crime rate that extends from the mobsters running the drug mafia to the petty thieves who roam the city slashing open pockets and purses.

In Latin America, one expects to live dangerously. That is part of Latin life.

A friend told me a story about a missionary couple who had their car stolen in this capital. A week after the incident they received a call from a person claiming to be the larcenist.

The caller expressed his shame at stealing from a Christian couple engaged in God's work.

The man appeared genuinely upset and eager to make amends to the missionaries. Not only was he prepared to return the vehicle, but was determined to make proper compensation for the inconvenience caused.

The caller said that he would like the couple to nominate their favourite restaurant. He would arrange a dinner for them, at his expense, and park their vehicle outside for their collection.

Keen to retrieve the car, the missionaries went along with the plan. They named the evening and the restaurant.

Unconvinced of the validity of the offer, they checked the day before with the restaurant owner. Sure enough, a booking had been made and confirmed by a generous financial payment.

With new faith in humanity, the two went to dinner. The car was parked outside as promised and both enjoyed a hearty meal.

On their way home they expressed their hope that the mystery caller would make contact again so that they could pass on their personal thanks.

However, there was no need. When they returned home they

found that their entire home had been stripped of all furnishing, jewellery and valuables.

'Don't even walk the main tourist drag in Bogota', I was told. 'Choose a cafe near your hotel.'

I was invited to have supper with a member of the human rights and research group CINEP (Centre for Investigation and Population) operated by the Society of Jesus, out of the Jesuit University, Bogota.

Father Carlos Vasco had set up the meeting at his office on the university campus.

As I was to discover, supper would be served at his home, which he explained was within walking distance.

We talked and walked and without noticing it we left behind the campus and the huge affluent town-houses, and stepped into a black void. The warnings about walking Bogota's streets at night flashed across my mind, but the priest appeared to have no concern. He was busily speaking about the exorbitant prices the rich were paying for these town-houses, while an escalating number of people were moving in from the rural areas to huge sprawling slums that surrounded the city.

We paused at the highway, ablaze with headlights from an unbroken stream of cars. The Jesuit remarked that this highway was the local Monte Carlo speedway. It was the demarcation line between the haves and have-nots of Bogota.

Holding hands we both made a break between the speeding cars and crossed into another city.

Each day crowds of children lead their donkeys across this motorway *en route* to the cafes and restaurants to collect the scraps. The waste is used to feed hungry families and pigs. Many of the youngsters and their faithful donkeys are killed by the traffic. But the authorities have not thought it important enough to install a bridge or traffic signals. Why invest in safety measures? The rich have no reason to cross this motorway.

Behind us a myriad of lights marking Bogota: in front of us pitch blackness, except for a great shadowy shape that the moon was attempting to spotlight.

This was hardly the night stroll that some of my colleagues in Bogota would recommend. But maybe there was nothing to fear. We were returning to Father Carlos' other world. The shadowy shape looming up before me was a hillside, where the Jesuits' community of friends lived, in houses perched like pigeon holes on the rugged slopes. We parted from the sealed footpath and began, with some difficulty, to climb the loose shale. Every now and then a flickering light could be seen. The thick hot air suddenly changed from deadly exhaust fumes to the choking smell of charcoal fires. Faces in the night would appear, then voices would be audible — nothing threatening, only friendly greetings between priest and parishioner. Sometimes a figure would fall in beside us and strike up a conversation. Carlos Vasco would indicate that this person had some community concern to share with him.

Who then would harm us, as we stumbled our way up this Colombian shanty-town hillside? We were probably much safer here than walking along the main tourist streets of downtown Bogota.

Father Carlos' house was here in this slum barrio, known as Sucre-Hero. One hundred and twenty families lived in primitive shanties.

A noise to my left attracted my attention. A small boy appeared out of the darkness, coaxing his weary donkey to continue up the last metres of the rocky track. Heavily laden leather bags hung to the sides of the animal. Already, the scraps of food from the tables of the rich Colombians had begun to sour and let off an offensive odour. Nevertheless this food would grace other tables and fill other empty bellies.

Beyond Sucre-Hero was San Martin barrio where 100 families lived, and beyond that still more slums where hundreds of families attempted to eke out an existence.

There were no government services in places like Sucre-Hero. The people were too poor to worry about. As a consequence of this poverty and government neglect, the barrio people had come together as a community under Father Carlos and his team of Jesuits.

The people had formed a working party and dug a crude sewerage system. Underground pipes fed into a central canal, which weaved its way down the hillside. Father Carlos used to strip to the waist after Sunday Mass and wield a pick along with the others.

'This sanitation is a lot better than we had before', remarked the priest.

Water remained a problem too. A couple of taps served the whole barrio. The water was badly polluted, but the Jesuits like everybody else had no other choice but to drink it. Father Carlos smiled and explained that he was too busy to take a sample of the water and put it under a microscope at the university. 'Maybe that was wise,' he continued.

The poor were not supplied with electricity, even though the power lines stretched over their hillside.

Once, a community meeting decided that this barrio was as much entitled to electricity as the people in the neighbouring penthouses. Miraculously, some daredevils had tapped into the overhead system and brought illegal currents into Sucre-Hero.

Periodically, the authorities would come around and cut off the power supply. Not daunted by these acts of officialdom, the community would wait until the inspectors were safely on the other side of the Monte Carlo speedway, then they would re-group their daredevils and Sucre-Hero would again be plugged into the electricity system.

The priest showed me a small shack on the hillside, explaining that it was through an incident here that the community came to understand that as a group they had to defend their rights.

An old woman, a squatter, had lived in the shack for years. Nobody claimed ownership of the property, and as a result she lived there undisturbed.

Without warning a businessman from the other side appeared, claiming to be the owner of the plot of ground.

The man knew how the poor generally react. They are so often humiliated by the appearance of someone of power, and creep off without more than a whimper.

But this landlord received more than he reckoned on. He was to discover that the woman was not prepared to vacate the property on the date that he had set. The landlord called in the police to evict her forcibly. On arrival, the constabulary found not just an old lady, but 120 families and Father Carlos surrounding the shack. The community refused to move — so the police quit. When they returned with reinforcements, the police found the community still there and still outnumbering the law. The police knew that they had lost that round. They went. The old woman stayed.

However, the incident did not go unnoticed. The police reported the blockade to their superiors, who carried the story to senior government officials, who in turn told the archbishop that it was a shame that priests did not carry out the ministry for which they were ordained.

This and other developments in the barrio resulted in the Society of Jesus being placed under surveillance by the security police and the church officialdom too.

The Jesuits had moved into Sucre-Hero in 1975. Father Carlos brought with him some seminarians. He reasoned that if these young men were to serve God's poor as priests, then living with God's poor was an essential part of their training. This identification would have greater impact on the poor than any catechesis or theology.

The experiment did not work.

The hierarchy of the archdiocese found that a slum setting was a totally unsatisfactory environment for young men. They needed the security of a seminary. Pressure was applied to the Society of Jesus and the young men were withdrawn. Most became disillusioned and left the order.

Then the hierarchy asked for the priests to be pulled out. But the superior of the Jesuits refused and argued for their retention. In some situations, the involvement of the Jesuits with the poor had led to bishops cancelling some priests' licences to celebrate the Mass.

What then is so objectionable about the ministry of people like Carlos Vasco?

They protect the powerless from the powerful by sharing the mind of Christ and making the powerless realise that they, too, are protected by rights.

What does it say to the rich Colombian Catholic when a priest goes to live with the poor, digs sanitation ditches, and confronts police officers who are called to evict illegal squatters? Colombia has honoured its clergy as members of the elite, upholders of the law of the country and sometimes pacifiers of the poor.

We sat in Father Carlos' tiny three-roomed shack, which he shares with three other Jesuits, and drank coffee. I could see the whole development pattern evolving. A community had been built, problems were being confronted, and change was beginning to happen.

Each morning Carlos Vasco crosses back into his world of academia. There, the priest meets a different branch of the human family. He spends some of his day celebrating Mass and counselling the students. Hopefully, the Jesuit will impart love and concern and a sense of justice into the potential leaders of tomorrow.

Later that night, back in downtown Bogota, I asked a friend: 'Couldn't these priests serve the needs of the poor as effectively by visiting the slums, but living in the Jesuit house on the university campus? Is there a real need to subject oneself to such raw poverty?'

My friend replied: 'They are no longer visitors to the poor. They are part of the community of the powerless. The Society of Jesus is looked upon as the intellectuals of the church, holy but proud men.

'What do you think it does to any illiterate family whose religious understanding is simplistic, when a Jesuit comes to your barrio and asks permission to live with your people and become your servant?

'Look at Sucre-Hero and see the results — no wonder the state and the church leaders are terrified.'

Here is my servant whom I uphold,
my chosen one in whom my soul delights.
I have endowed him with my spirit
that he may bring true justice to the nations.

He does not cry out or shout aloud,
or make his voice heard in the streets.
He does not break the crushed reed,
nor quench the wavering flame.

Faithfully he brings true justice;
he will never waver nor be crushed
until true justice is established on earth
for the islands are waiting new law.
— **Isaiah 42 — The first song of the suffering servant.**

Picota jail in Bogota. Inside this place there is unbelievable suffering and injustice. Here, human beings are cast into the pit of despair and wretchedness.

CHAPTER IV

COLOMBIA

Condemned to the Pits of Picota

The siege was continuing at the Dominican Embassy in Bogota, Colombia. A group of diplomatic staff, representing a number of Latin American nations, had been held hostage in this embassy for weeks by members of a Colombian guerilla movement, the M19.

The rebels were demanding the release of some of their colleagues who were being held in prisons around the country, including nearby Picota jail.

Neither the Colombian Government nor the M19 was prepared to compromise. So the drama dragged on. The international media had begun to lose interest and, it would seem, so too had most of the people of Bogota.

However, the events at the Dominican Embassy were very much on my mind that March morning in 1980.

I was in the office of a Baptist pastor, Don Rendle, and his wife, Georgie. The Canadian couple had been missionaries in Colombia since 1974, and were actively engaged in prison ministry. They had spread their love and concern to over 30 prisons.

One of the 30 jails was Picota, a deplorable disease-infested warren where criminals, the innocent and the mentally insane were cast. The Rendles had invited me to meet the prisoners and discover for myself the inhuman conditions in which these people lived. The pastor was hoping that World Vision could extend its community development programs into this God-forsaken place.

Picota was not difficult to visit, particularly if you were a guest of the Rendles. You could expect to have the commander of the prison guards personally escort you around.

However, today was different. I might not be the only visitor. The media was beginning to refocus its attention on the Dominican Embassy.

The Rendles were blunt. The weeks of stalemate had festered into deep frustration. The guerillas were going on a new attack. If their fellow rebels were not going to be released, then the M19 was prepared to storm its way in and free its companions.

'That could be today,' explained Don Rendle. 'It could happen while we are inside.'

I pictured the chaos if that should happen. From my understanding of similar situations it would be an opportunity for revengeful bloodletting.

The choice was mine. Today would be another day of ministry for the Rendles, M19 threats or not.

In situations like this, I gain new courage from the God of the poor, who never seems very far away from you.

Picota was not the first prison I had visited in the Third World, but as I was to discover, it was the worst. Like most of Latin America's jails it was grossly overcrowded (built to house 66 inmates but now choking its system with 1500), a tortuous hole totally unfit for human habitation. Today, it had another ghoulish addition.

Soldiers, decked out in full battledress, strutted around, displaying a more sinister appearance than the blue-uniformed guards at the gates and on the walls.

The troops questioned the wisdom of the commander of the guards after he gave us the all clear to enter. The soldiers viewed us with suspicion. I wondered if their concern had anything to do with our safety if an attack did occur, or whether they believed that we might be part of the attack itself.

Inside, I could expect to meet prisoners ranging from murderers to priests and police officers. In Colombia one could be jailed on another's allegation and it was the responsibility of the accused to prove his innocence.

For the rich, it was relatively easy. They would hire a good lawyer and have the charges heard in court. But legal fees were something that the poor could not afford. Therefore, many poor people were left in this depressing sink of humanity, the victims of personal vendettas.

The church has been frequently criticized for its lack of pastoral care in places like this. Somebody earlier that day warned me that apart from the Rendles, I would see no other Christian presence, particularly from the nation's dominating church — 'the Roman Catholics'.

The commander led us to an isolated group of buildings, some distance from the main complex.

My introduction to Picota was the tuberculosis hospital, morbid by Australian standards, yet one of the bright corners of the prison.

In a large stone assembly hall, a pathetic group of men ambled about. Catching sight of the visitors, they moved forward as close as they could to us. A roof-to-floor iron grille divided them from us.

Before me was a line of pinched white faces, pressed hard against this metal enclosure. It was a rueful sight to see these figures standing behind the giant cage.

Amidst this gloom, there was love and concern. These men were being nursed by a handful of St Vincent de Paul nuns. So my friend's comment was incorrect. The dominant church did have a presence here.

In spite of the crude surroundings the sisters were providing medical help. They had put together a very basic medical clinic. There were few provisions. One sister told me that soap was a luxury that they could not afford. The few pieces of equipment in the hospital looked as though they had been picked up from a dump. Like the people they were caring for, these nuns appeared to have been forgotten by the outside world.

The men behind the grille began disappearing, returning a few minutes later with both hands protruding between the bars. One hand clutched dolls' furniture, polished boxes and jewellery. The other was extended in welcome.

'These people are looking for a market to sell these goods,' explained Georgie. 'One of the tortures of being in this place is wondering what has become of your family. Most of these men might have had only a couple of days' employment a week. So the family lived in abject poverty. Now even that has been cut off.

'What becomes of the wife and children?'

'Too often the wife is forced into prostitution. Then the children are locked up in a humpy for up to 15 hours a day while the mother attempts to make a little money to feed them.'

The Rendles told me that the thought of a wife working in prostitution and the children neglected for long periods each day nearly tore these men apart. They were trapped, frequently with the knowledge that they were here only because somebody was seeking revenge.

As we spoke, the hands of welcome remained extended waiting for me to respond. Ten, fifteen, maybe twenty hands. I hesitated. These men were sick. Their hands were dirty. So I collected all the reasons why I should not touch the hands of these people. Then Georgie, who was rather attractive and very smartly dressed, did what should come naturally for someone who professes to love the poor. She walked over and gently held each hand and spoke to the patients about their families and their handcrafts.

When Georgie stepped back, the hands remained outstretched, beckoning the stranger to come forward. Reluctantly I approached the grille. As I touched this row of hands and saw their smiling faces, my hesitation passed to shame and then to consolation.

When I passed from the TB hospital to the main prison complex, I witnessed the extreme expression of injustice.

Men were crowded into a caged yard, similar to a dog pound, where human dignity was gradually wrung out of them and replaced by bitterness and brutality.

But travel down another laneway in this prison maze and you discover the gross imbalance between rich and poor.

Rather than being confined to a dog pound, the rich whiled away their enclosed days and weeks almost, but not quite, at home away from home.

For the enterprising businessman, a sentence at Picota provides an opportunity to open a branch office. In the midst of this human hell, the rich operated hairdressing salons, tailoring shops and restaurants where men sat around and grew fat on fine dishes and choice Colombian coffee.

On the streets of Bogota this disparity between lifestyles was scandalous. Inside Picota it was profoundly obscene.

This endless journey through Picota did have its moments of relief. Some of the prisoners were employed in trade work, while others were engaged in making handcrafts.

The commander of the guards continued down yet another musty passageway. We seemed to be walking deeper into the ground. The walls were damper and there appeared to be no further cells or signs of life. We stopped at a heavy iron door. The commander signalled one of his men to open it.

Somebody told me that we were about to visit the jail's insane asylum. The heavy door was shoved open. What we had already seen was depressing but this was difficult to describe. It seemed to me to be like a scene out of a Dickensian novel — a jail within the bowels of a jail.

Here, in this asylum, there was no feeling of violence or tension, only a horrible silence, as groups of men shuffled around a courtyard, with torn and filthy rags clinging to their bodies.

Some were crawling out of a concrete pit which the Rendles explained was a crude form of lavatory.

'These are the outcasts,' explained Don Rendle. 'Nobody comes in here except the guards. The food is only slop and is often heavily drugged to keep these people quiet.'

I watched these men. I had never seen poverty in this form before. They were absolutely neglected by the authorities and because of their physical condition, were unable to care for themselves.

One rather stout man walked up to our group. He was clad in an overcoat that was rotting on his body. It was being held together with some string. His white skin was black with filth. His fingernails were thick and clawed like a large bird. He

33

spoke only one word of English which he continued to repeat: 'Dollar, dollar . . .'.

Another, a tall man, also in rags, pushed him away. He stumbled to one side.

Our host, the commander, had moved away to find a splinter of sunshine at the other end of the compound.

Like a herd of cows, the men gradually moved in on us from all sides. Some mumbling; others silent; all staring at this collection of strange individuals. The little man was again begging for dollars.

For the second time today I felt totally inadequate. What could I do? I could not even offer them a word of comfort. How does one bring relief into an inhuman garrison like this?

I remembered the M19. If they did blast their way in, it might allow these people to escape from this wretched place.

Now I was aware of them, all around me, staring and begging.

Georgie showed me once more who I was and where I was.

I was in the presence of Christ and he had given me a rare privilege. I stood before his poor, the ones he so often spoke about.

Georgie carried on a long conversation in Spanish with the group around her.

We moved on further. I was yet to see the worst. Georgie led me into a long narrow room, a dormitory. Men lay motionless on bunk beds. Some were groaning. The smell was overpowering. The room was putrid. The threadbare blankets were held together by thick layers of grime. Many of the patients appeared unable to lift themselves off their rancid beds.

Georgie whispered that when these men became troublesome, the guards locked them away in individual cages.

Before we reached the iron gate that led back into the main complex, one of the patients hurried over to Georgie and put his hand on her shoulder. She did not attempt to shake it off. She stopped and listened to his excited speech.

'He is an old soldier and is recalling his days in combat. He wants to know what has happened to his family,' said Georgie.

When the man finished, we walked through the gate, which swung shut behind us. That part of Picota disappeared.

I walked on in silence, unable to forget the scene I had just witnessed. I remembered the willingness of Georgie to touch and listen to one of the most pathetic of God's creatures.

As we went on, Georgie spoke about her ministry, how she carried messages from prisoners to their families and how new family links were established. She told me about Wednesdays, when the prostitutes were allowed in to certain sections, and how venereal disease spread unchecked throughout the jail.

As I collected my camera at the main gates and walked back to the car, I asked the Rendles about some small wooden structures by the roadway.

'This is where wives and other members of the families are searched before they are allowed to go inside. Often male guards are called in to check the women when the queues become too long. The women are frequently indecently assaulted. But they have to put up with that treatment if they want to go inside and see their husbands,' said Georgie.

The food is so poor that the women will frequently prepare a favourite dish for their menfolk.

'The guards will often ask if there is anything hidden in the food. The women will assure the guards that it is only food. But many officials will drive a stick through the food, churning it up into a paste. The women must stand there and watch, their hearts broken while these bullies get their kicks.'

My visit to Picota is the subject of much personal reflection. The faces and hands at the grille. The cages crowded with men. And that yard deep in its bowels.

But most of all I remember Picota because it was there that I had to step out of the security of the crowd and own the disfigured Christ, who seemed no longer human, a thing despised and rejected.

There in the buried yard he left me speechless and showed and taught me many great things.

The Sovereign Lord has filled me
with his Spirit.
He has chosen me and sent me
to bring good news to the poor, to heal the broken-hearted,
to announce the release of captives,
and freedom to those in prison.
He has sent me to proclaim
that the time has come
when the Lord will save his people
and defeat his enemies.
He has sent me to comfort all who mourn.
The Lord says:
I love justice and hate oppression and crime.
— Isaiah 61: 1-2, 8.

More than a million Salvadorans have been displaced by the war and the campaign of terror against the church. Some are on the run in their country, others are refugees in another land. These Salvadorans are living in a refugee camp in Honduras.

CHAPTER V

EL SALVADOR

The Call

In the midst of Latin America's agony a new voice sounded.

It represented a bloc of people from diverse religious traditions, and as geographically distant as Brazil, El Salvador and the United States. Historically this bloc had been conspicuous by its silence. It drew its strength from conservative Catholicism and evangelical Protestantism.

The silent found a voice to protest. However, the protest was not directed at the repressive forces that harassed and killed the poor and those who challenged the structures that oppressed them. The new protest was levelled at the church of the poor, whom it claimed was being prostituted by the Marxists.

Even in far away Australia, I was accused by some fundamental Christian pastors of being a propagandist for the Communist side. They claimed that like the late Archbishop of San Salvador Oscar Romero and his supporters, I was being manipulated.

I was in Australia, they charged, and was unaware of how the Communists had infiltrated the Catholic Church, the Christian Base Communities and particularly the Society of Jesus, the Jesuits. These fundamentalists claimed that the left had misled Oscar Romero, who had been willing to use his cathedral pulpit as a political platform.

On one point, the fundamentalists were correct. I was dependent on infrequent telephone conversations and second-hand reports for my information. There was a gap between the reality of what was happening in Central America and my understanding of it in a safe and comfortable Australia.

The communications director of World Vision, Philip Hunt, a close colleague of mine, bridged that gap.

Philip Hunt asked me if I would be prepared to go to El Salvador to report on World Vision's work and try to gain some first-hand information about that troubled country.

There was no doubt in my mind. I was prepared to leave immediately. However, Hunt, a very sensitive person, sought further approval from my wife, Nain. This was 1982; the violence was still at its peak. Not long afterwards I was on my way to El Salvador.

My deepest reflections on El Salvador were while flying there via the United States. Going over the wide Pacific, one has plenty of time to think.

For the first time I felt a little fearful. Was this a wise decision? I had left behind a wife and five children. What could I possibly do that would help the Salvadorans? If the death squads had been prepared to silence an archbishop, they would have no hesitation in dealing with me.

Overseas airliners give me a much needed period to pray and listen to God. I was *en route* to a people who had deeply inspired me and that was final. I put my life in the hands of God, settled back in my seat and thanked Him for this privilege. Already too much had happened not to believe that God was directing me along a certain course. And the chain of events which would get me into El Salvador strengthened my sense of being under his hand.

First of all, time and aircraft connections were crucial.

World Vision had chosen my flight times because its staff in San Salvador had indicated that there was a lull in the violence.

But to fly into San Salvador International Airport and travel the 45 minutes of highway back into the capital was out of the question. There were constant guerilla ambushes on that highway, and anyway who would be safe travelling along this road patrolled by security forces who were as much a hazard as the guerillas?

Arrangements were made for me to fly from Los Angeles to

Guatemala City. Here I was to meet up with some colleagues from World Vision's Latin American regional office, and after a short briefing fly into San Salvador's old airport in the capital city. We had been given special clearance to do this because we represented an international aid agency. The flight schedules were in place and times and dates could not be changed.

At the immigration desk at Guatemala City airport an official checked my tourist card and passport. He looked up at me and in his broken English informed me that I was not able to enter Guatemala. Astonished, I asked why?

'You do not have a proper visa. This is only a tourist card. You need a visa', he replied.

I explained that Australia's Department of Foreign Affairs, Qantas Airlines, and Pan Am had all advised me that a tourist card was all I needed.

The immigration officer shook his head and said: 'No good. You will have to return to Los Angeles to get a proper visa.'

This Australian had come too far to turn back now. I argued that I represented an international humanitarian agency and had come from Australia to carry out an urgent assignment. The reply was still negative.

I demanded to see his superior. I was led like a fugitive down a series of passageways to a small dingy office. A group of men sat on the sides of desks and began asking me a variety of questions. It appeared that they were more interested in the life and job opportunities in Australia than helping me get through the immigration gate.

A serious-faced official entered, checked my passport and travel card and firmly announced that I would have to fly back to Los Angeles. At the same time, he summoned a local Pan Am representative and in Spanish demanded to know why the airline had flown me into this country without proper documentation.

Apologetically the Pan Am man told me it was his company's error and it would gladly fly me back to the US to collect the correct visa. He said that I should be able to complete the documentation and be back in Guatemala within 48 hours. The vital flight to El Salvador left in just 12 hours, and there was no telling when, or if, another could be arranged.

Despite my protests the discussions came to an abrupt end. I made one final, desperate attempt to save my trip to El Salvador. I asked to speak to my Guatemala office, hoping against hope that World Vision would have some solution. Finally my persuasive powers won through. At the other end of a noisy line, the World Vision field director of Guatemala appeared more amused than concerned. He said something about knowing one of the regime's generals, then suggested that if the plane on which I'd arrived was making its round trip via Costa Rica, he would contact the World Vision office there and see if they could arrange to have a visa ready for me.

My chances of flying into El Salvador first thing in the morning were quickly diminishing. Anyhow, Latin American embassies don't work that fast. It was most unlikely that the visa would be waiting for me in Costa Rica.

I replaced the receiver feeling rather dejected. The immigration official smiled and wished me all the best. The Pan Am representative, still apologizing, led me back up the maze of passages. My life had been put into God's hands. Maybe this was a message to me. Perhaps I was really seeking high adventure, rather than seeking to do His work.

I was escorted back onto the Pan Am Boeing 707. The same cabin crew smiled as if to welcome me back. The engines began to turn over and the aircraft taxied along the tarmac ready for its flight to Costa Rica.

At the end of the runway the engines burst into a roar. I looked over the lights of Guatemala City. Then there was a sudden hush. The engines slowed to a hum. From the flight deck came the captain's voice.

'We have just been advised from the flight tower that there has been a blackout at San Jose airport, Costa Rica. We are returning to the terminal to await further instructions. Please remain in your seats. We will not be disembarking because we hope to be taking off in a few minutes.'

Back at the terminal we waited. Word came through that emergency lighting was being set up at San Jose airport and we would be taking off in a few moments.

I noticed that the aerobridge was being pushed out to the

plane. Then the aircraft door opened. The same apologetic Pan Am representative came running down the aisle.

'Mr Philp, Mr Philp. Please follow me. The officials have changed their minds. You can stay.'

I could not believe it as I followed him along the aisle past the bewildered cabin crew. As we walked down the terminal corridor towards the immigration gate the Pan Am man told me he was a lay member of the Salesian order. Tomorrow he would be off to lead a boys' camp and he would be telling them of God's influence in the world: the Guatemalan officials had tried to prevent me coming into the country to do my humanitarian work, but God had stopped the plane.

The Pan Am official had no idea why the change of heart. At the gate the same immigration official checked my passport, tore up my tourist card and stamped in my book — tourist visa. He signalled me through.

Outside I was greeted by a good friend from the World Vision office.

'We thought we had missed you. I drove to the airport to tell you that you are able to stay but was told that the plane had gone. Thank Heavens for the blackout', smiled Dina.

'But why did the officials change their minds so quickly?', I asked.

'Our field director knows one of the generals here', replied the World Vision woman.

I do not believe that God is in the business of stopping aeroplanes or finding parking spots in busy shopping centres. However, I do believe that when He calls us to follow Him and we respond positively then we can confidently leave it to Him to see us safely through the journey.

Call to me and I will answer you; I will tell you great mysteries of which you know nothing. For this is what Yahweh, the God of Israel, says about the houses in this city and the royal palaces of Judea which are to be destroyed.
— Jeremiah 33: 3-4.

Thousands of Salvadorans and many overseas visitors packed the square outside the Metropolitan Cathedral for the funeral service of Archbishop Romero in 1980. An altar was placed on the cathedral steps for the celebration of the Mass. However, the Mass was suddenly thrown into chaos when bombs exploded and people were cut down by gunfire. Nobody claimed responsibility. It is believed that the military opened fire on the crowd from a nearby government building.

The banners read:
'With the Salvadorian people in its greatest struggle.
With the people for its final liberation.'
'The truth will make us free'.

CHAPTER VI

EL SALVADOR

In the City of the Saviour

I have never before been introduced to a country by being taken off an airliner, and rushed to a hotel room to undergo a thorough briefing lasting nearly two hours. Amongst other things, I was warned that my telephone could be tapped. My movements were likely to be monitored. Car registration plates would probably be recorded if our vehicle was parked near certain locations.

But this was not a normal environment. I was in El Salvador in 1982. This is the country named after the Great Liberator of the poor and the oppressed: El Salvador, the nation of Jesus Christ, the Saviour of the world. For centuries the Gospel of Christ has been proclaimed here. Ninety per cent of the people claim to believe in Christ — the Prince of Peace.

Yet now there was a morbid atmosphere hanging over the republic. The Saviour of the world had been terrorised. He had been butchered behind eerie walls. His body had been dumped on garbage heaps.

Today the sinister death squads ruled in Christ's city, San Salvador.

My briefing was conducted by a former Salvadoran senator. His party once formed a coalition with the left, but he quit politics, frustrated by a series of electoral frauds and constant threats on his life from the ruling elite. Now he was helping the poor through an aid program.

As he warned me about the dangers that I might face in the next few days, I could detect the fear that this man carried within himself. I asked him about his own situation. He told me that the security forces were killing their way through all known opposition political figures in a systematic fashion. A military colleague had warned him that his name had been mentioned as a suspected subversive.

University lists were being studied for the same reason. Professors and students who had shown some anti-government feeling or had written a thesis supporting a labour movement or Leftist personality, maybe five or ten years ago, were being earmarked for assassination.

He warned that only the courageous mentioned the name of Oscar Romero.

Nobody slept soundly in El Salvador. The ex-senator told me that recently a death squad arrived in his street. It was after midnight. He, like his neighbours, knew who it must be when the vehicle ground to a halt. From 10pm to 6am there was curfew. Nobody went out on the streets and broke curfew, because the national guard shot on sight.

'When the wagon stopped and voices were heard, we knew that the night visitors were not the national guard. They rarely stopped. I said to my wife: "Is it our turn? Maybe it's Jose next door — or it could be Juan's family further down the street".'

It was not the ex-senator's turn that night. However, the squad had forced its way into another house and murdered the family.

Next morning the press reported that the family were known subversives and had opened fire on security officers. So concluded the story. There would be no further investigations.

The ex-senator was prepared to flee at a moment's notice. He knew he was living on borrowed time. There was still the fear that despite his emergency arrangements the squad would get him first. In the meantime, he continued to assist the poor through his organisation.

My first evening in El Salvador was spent with a Protestant community who served the poor in the capital city.

The political polarisation that was making deep wounds in Salvadoran society had also carved new divisions into the Body of Christ.

This nation, like most in Latin America, has a very bitter sectarian past, where the Catholic Church has been the elephant and the various Protestant denominations, the mice. Both Spanish Catholicism and North American Protestantism have deep conservative roots.

In addition to this scandalous division, a new gulf developed dividing those brothers and sisters representing mainstream Protestantism from those who called themselves evangelical Protestants.

The community I was with that evening had made a courageous stand with the poor. Its leaders had been invited by the Salvadoran Government to enjoy some of the privileges that the State had withdrawn from the Catholic Church. Following his conversion and in the face of escalating repression, Oscar Romero had cut all church links with the State. The government's hand of friendship to the evangelicals resulted from this action.

The forty pieces of silver that the national president was offering to the Protestant churches meant visas for missionaries, land for churches, and support for evangelistic crusades. All of this was theirs if they were prepared to preach a Gospel that did not threaten the status quo.

This Protestant community walked out and had gone instead to the office of Archbishop Romero and pledged their support in the struggle to bring the good news of God's justice to the poor.

That action had identified them as anti-government. The State would list them as leftists and so would many of their fellow Protestants. The new direction they were taking brought them alongside a new branch of the Christian family, Catholic brothers and sisters who were traditionally strangers to them.

As we sat in the bare but substantial church these Christians spoke about members of their youth group.

'Three young brothers from our church were thrown into prison. The police claimed they were subversives and were collaborating with terrorists. They were accused of taking food to guerillas. But the truth was they were taking food to refugees camped at another church.'

47

The pastor told me how the Christian churches in El Salvador, Sweden, Britain and the US had written to the government pleading for the release of these young people.

'After this international pressure the army demanded a ransom of $1200 for their release. We could not afford that sum, so the army accepted a smaller amount. After being tortured and held in detention without charges for three months, the brothers were released', said the pastor.

Soon after this community had begun working with the poor and making them aware of their human rights, two members of the congregation were murdered, another disappeared and two ordained ministers had to leave the country after they were warned that their names were on a death squad hit list.

The new-found unity with the Catholics had been carefully watched. The Protestants started a vocational training program among the unemployed with a neighbouring Catholic parish. As a result, the Catholic priest was killed and the life of the senior pastor of the Protestant church was threatened.

Each time there was a noise outside, I could see these Christians suddenly tense up as though they were expecting some mad gunman to burst in and shoot them. Only recently one of their church members, a medical doctor, had disappeared. They told me that he had apparently treated somebody who belonged to the other side.

We were on the road back to my hotel soon after 8.30pm. It was still some time before curfew, but my guide explained that some of the national guard did not own watches. Any time after dark was good enough for the soldiers to declare curfew.

The streets were almost deserted. One or two taxis sped along taking home their last fares. The atmosphere was frightening in this darkened and empty city.

My guide stopped at a set of red traffic lights. Crazy, I thought. He was eager to get off the streets and yet here we were waiting at an intersection without another vehicle in sight. As we waited a shape appeared out of the shadows. A large armoured vehicle emerged, carrying the infamous national guard in their dark uniforms.

They were beginning another night of patrolling these

streets, 'protecting' the civilian population from any unexpected guerilla attack. However, they would blindly ignore their colleagues in the vehicles that ground to a halt outside particular homes. The national guard never saw the other night predators — the death squads.

Arriving back at my hotel, I was suddenly confronted by noise, lights and music.

The international media, a collection of business executives, and presumably some local Salvadoran elite were gathered around the pool singing, dancing and making merry, apparently oblivious to the other world that surrounded them.

San Salvador is an extraordinary place.

I can see how violence
and discord fill the city;
day and night they stalk together
along the city walls.

Sorrow and misery live inside, ruin is an inmate;
tyranny and treachery are never absent
from its central square.

Unload your burden onto Yahweh,
and he will support you;
he will never permit the virtuous to falter.

As for those murderous, those treacherous men,
You, God, will push them
down to the deepest pit
before half their days are out.
— Psalm 55: 10-11; 22-23.

Archbishop Arturo Rivera y Damas celebrating Mass on the anniversary of the martyrdom of the four United States missionaries, Maura Clarke, Ita Ford, Jean Donovan and Dorothy Kazel. The four women were murdered by the Salvadoran National Guard.

CHAPTER VII

EL SALVADOR

Priests of the Poor

Some of the most meaningful hours I spent in El Salvador were with the people to whom I had spoken on the telephone, courageous Christians who had risked their lives to tell me the truth about their country.

Now I could sit with them and share face to face. Meeting them like this only increased my admiration for them.

The priest to whom I had most frequently spoken by telephone welcomed me. I introduced myself for the first time by name. He seemed very interested to hear that I was from Australia. He told me of his fellow priests who had been assassinated and about his very close colleagues who had been forced into exile.

Our conversation was interrupted by the phone ringing. After a few moments he put down the receiver and explained that the caller was the provincial of the Maryknoll order in El Salvador. Five Maryknoll priests were being forced to leave the country because the military had threatened their lives.

He was also concerned about Radio YSAX, the independent Catholic radio station. In recent days its transmitters had been bombed yet again. The church had managed to bring some new equipment into the country, but the customs department was refusing to release it.

He pointed to a letter on his desk. It was from a union representing seven communities. The group was not connected with the left, in fact it had tended to be pro-government. The union had written to him and to the defence minister asking why the

Salvadoran national guard was killing its members.

The priest paused and then said to me: 'Before we preach at any Mass we must carefully think about what the Gospel is saying and remind ourselves that it could mean martyrdom for us'.

He then spoke about the bold way Archbishop Oscar Romero preached the Word of God, knowing that he was signing his own death warrant.

'He knew he would die. But we are not all Romeros. I am afraid. I admit I do not speak like Romero. I believe in him and his witness, but maybe I do not have the strength to face death like him', continued the priest.

I spoke with the priest about the inspiration that he and other members of the church had been to me. He seemed surprised.

'We are not doing anything special. We are only trying to be faithful to the Gospel', he replied.

When I began to make my farewells, an amazing thing happened. As he clutched my hand, the priest said: 'Another Australian sometimes rings me from your country'.

It suddenly dawned on me that when I was introduced to him as Peter Philp, the name meant nothing. He had welcomed me as a person representing World Vision. Excitedly I explained who I was. Now he realised that the Australian he had welcomed was the stranger in whom he had placed so much trust at the end of a distant telephone line over the past year. It was a significant and moving moment for both of us.

A Jesuit priest had also provided me with vital information during my monitored telephone calls. The most dangerous members of the church, in the eyes of the government and its armed forces, are the Jesuits. I had read about his denunciations of human rights and his challenge to the traditional, silent church that saw its sole ministry as celebrating the Mass and administering the Sacraments. Strangely, after years of publicly criticising this structure, the man was still alive.

Therefore when we sat down in an out-of-town Jesuit house, I could not help but ask him, 'Why aren't you dead?'.

He smiled and said: 'When the first attempt is made on your

life you cannot believe it. The second and third attempts make you frightened. After the thirteenth, you realise God doesn't want you to die.'

All this bloodshed, this conflict between rich and poor, is a by-product of a 50-year history in El Salvador that has allowed millions of peasants to exist under a repressive feudal system while a handful of rich oligarchs have lived in luxury.

'Some of the hierarchy (the oligarchy and the military) believe that they have been chosen to rule and that they own the chickens, the cows, and the peasants', explained the Jesuit.

He was adamant that the new awareness of the poor did not come out of Marxist or Leninist teaching. Knowledge about the dignity of man had been understood because God had reformed His church through Vatican II and the Medellin Bishop's Conference.

'The Catholic Church saw that the poverty, the starvation, the lack of health and education, did not depend on the will of the individual but was produced by the system.

'At Medellin, the church said that this basic economic system produces violence. This violence is institutionalised violence. This was especially true in the last two years of Oscar Romero's life. There was a tremendous increase in repression from the side, whatever you want to call it, the rightists. So hundreds of people started being killed. Now the numbers are in thousands, as you know', said the priest.

The Jesuit told me that the people of Salvador understand Jesus very well. He said they believe Jesus must have been like their murdered archbishop, and they are now reading the Gospel with different eyes.

'They know that in El Salvador or in Guatemala, if a Christian tells the truth he is attacked or murdered. They (the people) read the Gospel and find answers which have always been there but for centuries they have not understood it.

'If they are taught God loves the poor, they read the Gospel and see it there. "The Kingdom of God is for you, the poor". I think that the Bible in general has been influential in changing the minds and the world vision of Christians, especially the peasants', continued the priest.

'Recently in one of our catechetical classes the children were talking about the book of Genesis. The teacher asked them, "Who made the world?" They answered "God". The teacher asked "For whom did he make the world?". "For everyone", answered the children. "Do all the people share the world?" then asked the teacher. "No", said the children, "just a few".'

It is not an easy task to follow in the footsteps of a man who was a champion of the people, an international identity, a courageous Christian leader and a martyr.

When Pope John Paul II appointed a successor to Oscar Romero as Archbishop of San Salvador, Monsignor Arturo Rivera y Damas must have felt a heavy burden of responsibility and probably wondered how he was going to meet the extraordinary expectations the people had for their archbishop.

I do not believe that the church in El Salvador is disappointed with their new chief pastor. It is true, Arturo Rivera is not an Oscar Romero. Rivera is very definitely Rivera, as Romero was Romero. However, the new Archbishop of San Salvador walks closely with Jesus Christ who strengthened and inspired his predecessor.

The appointment of Rivera as archbishop was a courageous decision. When Archbishop Luis Chavez retired in 1977, the authorities and the rich Catholic landowners in El Salvador were concerned about the direction the church was taking. The old archbishop had attempted to reform his church in line with the teachings of Vatican II and the documents of the Latin American Bishops' Conference in Medellin.

There was tremendous pressure on the church to appoint a safe, conservative archbishop who would be able to apply the brakes to these reforms. But the people and the progressive clergy were looking to the only candidate who was likely to accelerate these reforms. That person was the Bishop of Santiago de Maria, Arturo Rivera y Damas. The final decision favoured the safe conservative and not the progressive. Oscar Romero became archbishop. However, he quickly dumbfounded his fellow priests and the Salvadoran authorities with a total turnaround in his own life.

There must have been great pressure on the church when it had to appoint a new Shepherd to replace the murdered Romero. Most of the Salvadoran bishops were committed to the status quo and enjoyed the privileges of state. But John Paul named the pastor who was a man of the poor and would guide his flock in the same spirit as Romero.

A few weeks before I met him in San Salvador, Archbishop Arturo Rivera y Damas had been threatened with death. A terror squad, identifying itself as the ESE, announced it was prepared to assassinate the archbishop and his auxiliary, Gregorio Rosa Chavez.

I asked the archbishop if he was concerned about the threat.

'Yes, we are human beings, but we are here to provide a service with generosity and honesty', he replied.

He spoke at length about the abuse of human rights in his country.

'Human rights', explained Monsignor Rivera, 'are universal rights. Every country should be interested in them, regardless of where these rights are being violated.'

As chief pastor of this suffering Christian nation, Monsignor Rivera described the situation as a process of ups and downs. 'There are weeks when you would say that matters are improving, but there are weeks when everything seems as though it is going to collapse. Our problems are permanent if the human rights situation is not solved', said the archbishop.

He placed the majority of the blame on the death squads. 'While they are there', he remarked, 'the problem is still there.'

I asked him what effect his powerful denunciation of this violence had on the death squads, presuming that the majority of them claimed some affiliation with his church.

He smiled and said: 'Their reaction is the threat they have made to kill me'.

Conservative Christians have often questioned the role of the church of the poor, claiming that there are guerilla priests, who carry arms and advance the cause of Marx and not Christ.

Yes, confirmed the archbishop, there are priests operating in territory that is held by the guerillas, but they are only carrying out priestly duties. 'They have gone there on their own initia-

55

tive', said Monsignor Rivera. He explained that he would never send them into guerilla country, not because he disapproved of their ministry, but because of the extreme danger to their lives. He told me that many guerilla areas were not held on a permanent basis and therefore there was constant confrontation with the army. If the zones were more stable under guerilla control, it would be different.

However, he is very aware that many of the guerillas are Christians who need pastoral care. He told me that the church suffers no harassment when it carries out its ministry in these guerilla areas and 'if a priest is willing to go in and help them it's okay'.

Another bishop once condemned these priests as men who had abrogated their ordination vows to become subversives. Archbishop Rivera has replied to this charge by saying that priests have the same duty to pastor to guerillas as chaplains had to pastor to the army.

Only social reform and not violence or military campaigns would provide his country with permanent solutions. Therefore he has condemned the killing and abuse of human rights by the guerillas too and encouraged them, as he has encouraged the government, to commit themselves to peace through dialogue and reconciliation so that a genuine liberation can occur.

I was reminded of this in a very powerful way the next Sunday when I attended his 8am Mass in the cathedral. It was broadcast nationwide by the Catholic radio station YSAX. Obviously his commitment to God and to his people was stronger than his fear of the ESE death squad. During his homily he denounced those who, during the past week, had killed and tortured his Salvadoran brothers and sisters. He called for solutions to his country's problems that were based on justice. He called for an end to foreign intervention. At the end of this courageous homily the packed cathedral congregation rose to its feet and applauded their bishop.

In spite of all the tension and persecution that Archbishop Rivera faces daily, there is an unmistakable peace about him.

How does he keep his faith and peace in this environment?

'When you have a good conscience that you are doing something to help God's people, you are at peace', answered the archbishop.

A World Vision colleague of mine who was present at this interview said: 'Monsignor, you are a courageous Christian'.

My life has been threatened many times. I have to confess that, as a Christian, I do not believe in death without resurrection. If they kill me, I will rise again in the Salvadoran people.

As a shepherd I am obliged by divine law to give my life for those I love, for the entire Salvadoran people, including those Salvadorans who threaten to assassinate me.

A bishop will die, but the Church of God, which is the people, will never perish.
— **Oscar Romero.**

This Salvadoran woman witnessed hideous crimes committed against her community. They killed her husband and the parish priest, and hanged small children.

CHAPTER VIII

EL SALVADOR

A Heaven in Hell

The most astonishing place I have ever visited is San Jose de la Montana.

It is the Catholic Diocesan Seminary for El Salvador. San Jose is a grand old college where young Salvadoran men study for the priesthood.

This stately edifice accurately demonstrates the image that traditional Catholicism had portrayed in Latin society. It is big, rich, and powerful.

Not only is the building structure of San Jose consistent with this portrait, but so too is its location. St Joseph of the Mountain seminary resides alongside the rich and powerful in San Salvador.

One could therefore understand the cries of hostility from bishops, generals, and the business establishment when they saw this holy sanctuary become, in their terms, a den for subversives, murderers, and the rabble of Salvadoran society.

It was Oscar Romero who opened the doors of the seminary to the terrified little people from the rural areas. These peasants had been hounded out of their Base Christian Communities by the army, the national guard, and paramilitary goon squads.

The archbishop also provided shelter in this seminary to the Co-Madres, the mothers of the missing. And buried in the cellars of this college, hammering away, are presses printing *Orientacion*, the Catholic journal and one of the few newspapers not under state control. Further along the hallway, announcers and control operators keep the voice of the Catholic radio station, YSAX, on the air. Both of these vital channels of news and information are amazing examples of survival and courage.

It was via YSAX that the famous Sunday homilies of Oscar Romero, and later Archbishop Arturo Rivera y Damas, were broadcast all over Salvador and throughout Central American nations. This was the voice that boldly exposed the week's atrocities being carried out by the security forces in the name of law and order.

During the late 70s and early 80s, security forces and terror squads burst into these cellars, smashed the printing press and bombed the radio transmitters.

As soon as the debris cleared, church workers would attempt to patch up presses and transmitters. Sometimes the broadcasting equipment was beyond repair. When the church tried to bring in new equipment to rebuild their radio station, the authorities would refuse to let it into the country. Christian El Salvador was using its might to prevent the proclamation of the Gospel. God's Good News to the poor was being effectively silenced.

After a series of long interruptions, ways and means and sheer determination finally put YSAX back on the air.

The courage of the journalists and editors at *Orientacion* and the announcers and programmers at YSAX made me feel proud of my profession.

However, San Jose de la Montana is not astonishing merely because of this newspaper and radio station in the cellars. What was both horrific and yet beautiful, were God's broken, scarred, and courageous disciples who had fled from their decimated communities to find shelter in the grounds of the seminary.

There have been many moments when I have been shattered by the sights and the stories of peasant people in Central America. I have felt like crying out to God, asking Him why He allowed His children to be butchered as if they were wild animals.

As I stepped through the flimsy wire gates at the side of the seminary, my doubts melted. The faith that I was struggling with was suddenly restored.

There I saw the suffering Christ — face to face. These people had escaped from their villages with few worldly possessions, but they had steadfastly refused to compromise their faith in the Holy Saviour. Simple though it might be, this faith was powerful enough to survive the most sadistic atrocities.

The seminarians at San Jose could no longer play soccer on their oval. Over a thousand peasant families, with the blessing of the church, had buried the grounds under a collection of cardboard and timber shanties. At first glance it looked hideous but after I had a chance to adjust my Western bias I realised I was part of a deeply moving Christian community.

At least now, I thought, these children of God were safe. But the camp director at San Jose shook his head. Not even here, in the Catholic seminary, could these frightened people live in peace.

Not long before my visit, one of the most brutal para-military squads, ORDEN, broke its way in.

The camp director told me that the squad attacked some of these displaced people. At that moment, Bishop Rivera y Damas * was inside the building speaking with the seminarians. He was alerted to the attack, and had he not used his position to have this armed mob called off, many of the people would have been killed.

The activities of this para-military group were so barbaric that at one time even the military dictator had ordered ORDEN to be outlawed. However, by the early '80s it had reappeared in public, carrying out the slaughter that even the regular army found difficult to perform.

One of the extraordinary people I met at San Jose was Theresa, who had fled from her home in San Vincente. She witnessed her father's murder by the national guard because he was an active member of the local Catholic Church.

Theresa lived on a small farm with her family. On six acres of ground they grew corn, rice and beans and were self-sufficient.

* In 1981, Rivera y Damas was Apostolic Administrator and not yet archbishop.

It was a very close community and the people were active members of their church.

Three months after the assassination of Theresa's father, the national guardsmen reappeared. They entered many homes including Theresa's. Her husband and four of her cousins were assassinated. The guard accused them of being members of a subversive church. The priest and the church people had been involved in community development, education, general awareness programs, and training people to understand their basic human rights.

The national guard took Theresa to its headquarters. She was held there for two days. Painfully she recalled how she was brutally bashed and raped. When left alone she managed to escape. ORDEN tracked her down and she was accused this time of collaborating with the left. Again she was bashed and raped.

By the grace of God, Theresa managed to escape again and hid in a nearby canyon. ORDEN tracked her movements and soon troops were swarming throughout the canyon. Theresa told me how they yelled death threats that echoed throughout the canyon. Eventually she scrambled out of this place. Under the cover of night she reached a house. It wasn't long before she heard ORDEN soldiers approaching. Again she fled, this time into a coffee plantation. 'Had it not been for this planta-tion', said Theresa, 'they would have captured and killed me.' Staggering out of the plantation she was grabbed by a man. God was with her. The man was a member of her local church.

He took her to his home and arranged for Theresa to be taken to the seminary. She was in a serious condition on her arrival and church authorities had to bring in a medical team to attend to her.

At the seminary she learned that later the national guard had come again to her village and killed her four brothers. Her children at least were safe and joined her at the seminary.

As she stood on the seminary soccer field clutching one of her children and gazing over the cardboard and timber camp, she said that she couldn't understand how a government would allow its soldiers to kill its own people. 'They want to kill everybody', she said.

Theresa's story is not unique or an isolated case. Most families at San Jose seminary can recall similar horrific stories.

Theresa hopes that the people will work together to help those who are suffering. She doubts whether she will live to see peace in El Salvador. However, she prays to God that her children will find peace.

In the same community was 12-year-old Domingo who saw the assassination of four members of his family. In his case the murderers weren't masked figures coming out of the night in civilian clothing. He saw national guardsmen, police, and members of ORDEN murdering his community.

Domingo told me that just before Christmas, a troop of perhaps 500 men arrived in his village. It was dark when they stormed into his house. His four brothers were grabbed and murdered before his eyes. Then these troops brought in his father and killed him. During this bloody raid, his mother and two sisters managed to escape. In the confusion Domingo ran too. The national guardsmen saw him and gave chase. He was seized and knocked to the ground. The guardsmen drew their machetes and carved up the boy: his neck, his skull, his arms and his fingers. His attackers left, believing that Domingo was dead.

He apparently lay on the ground for two days. When the military left the district, his mother crept back and found her son in a pool of blood, but still alive.

Domingo is now being cared for at the Catholic seminary. His deeply gashed body records forever the truth of what is happening in El Salvador.

Why did the troops burst into that village and murder four members of Domingo's family? His father and mother were members of a rural campesinos' group, a workers' union.

San Jose is a community where the crucified Christ lives with His people; cooks tortillas on the open fire with His people; washes His ragged clothes in the crude troughs with His people and shares the horrid nightmares with His people.

I love San Jose de la Montana. This is the place where I had the privilege of touching the Perfect Body — Jesus Christ.

Beware of men: they will hand you over to sanhedrins and scourge you in their synagogues. You will be dragged before governors and kings for my sake, to bear witness before them and the pagans. But when they hand you over, do not worry about how to speak or what to say; what you are to say will be given to you when the time comes; because it is not you who will be speaking, the Spirit of your Father will be speaking in you. Do not be afraid of them therefore. For everything that is now covered will be uncovered, and everything now hidden will be made clear. What I say to you in the dark, tell in the daylight; what you hear in whispers, proclaim from the housetops.
— **Matthew 10: 17-19, 26-27.**

P.RUTILIO GRANDE,S.J.
+ 12/3/77
LOS CAMPESINOS.

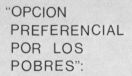

"OPCION
PREFERENCIAL
POR LOS
POBRES":

PUEBLA.

P.ALFONSO NAVARRO,D
+11/5/77
LOS ESTUDIANTES.

P.ERNESTO BARRERA
MOTTO,D.
+28/11/78
LOS OBREROS.

P.OCTAVIO ORTIZ LUNA,D.
+ 20/1/79
LOS JOVENES.

P.RAFAEL PALACIOS,D.
+20/6/79
LA COMUNIDAD.

P.ALIRIO NAPOLEON
MACIAS,D.
+ 4/8/79
LA SOLIDARIDAD.

'You can have no greater love than to lay down your life for your friends.' The turning point in Central America came when priests and pastors began dying for their people. They became a sign of inspiration to the people. They became a threat to those who wanted to keep the poor in bondage. These six pastors dared to live the commitment that the church made at Medellin and later endorsed at Puebla of making a preferential option for the poor.

CHAPTER IX

EL SALVADOR

A People Forging their own History

There must have been millions of tears shed, millions of prayers offered and millions of hearts broken in El Salvador. In spite of this, the guns relentlessly kill, the death squads constantly roam the cities and villages haunting the people, and mothers and children live with the perpetual nightmares of horror they have suffered and witnessed.

It is not only the internal godless lust for power that maintains this pathological madness. There are also external contributors: the paragons of democracy who manipulate Salvador through their foreign policy; the highly esteemed multinational corporations who arm the sadistic security forces and whose bloody returns pay their shareholders handsome dividends. And there are those of us who hold up the status quo by our silence.

While there is a serious responsibility to expose the injustices of this land, we must not negate the progress being achieved in the struggle for peace and justice.

The world must also hear the good news about the people and the events of El Salvador. Despite everything, new directions are being carved. There will be no turning back.

I will not forget the hot Friday morning when I climbed up the pitted steps of the metropolitan cathedral in San Salvador. Corrugated iron and green plastic sheets plugged up gaping holes over and around the towering entrance.

Today was December 2, and a group of priests were robing in an alcove near the front door.

People were streaming in to find a seat on the old discoloured pews. The rusting iron stanchions and scaffolding that scarred the outside of this great cathedral intruded into the interior roofline, side pillars, and inside walls as well. I glanced up at the stained glass windows, a feature of all famous cathedrals.

But San Salvador's were different. Rather than leadlight, there was more corrugated iron and green plastic.

Behind the main altar, massive sheets of old timber hid the huge empty shell of the yet-to-be-completed church.

At the last minute the archbishop, Arturo Rivera y Damas, hurried up the front steps and quickly pulled on his white alb and bishop's mitre. The priests shuffled into line ready to process up the aisle. Next to the archbishop was his vicar-general, the priest who had served Oscar Romero as vicar-general too, Monsignor Ricardo Urioste.

A nun, leading a small group of singers and musicians, began the entrance hymn. The only words I could pick up from the antiquated and distorting speakers were 'El Salvador'.

The archbishop and his people, mainly the very poor, had come together to celebrate Mass on the anniversary of the death of the four United States missionary women, martyred by the national guard on December 2, 1980.

This was a deeply spiritual experience. I was kneeling in worship with the people for whom these courageous women had given their lives. The chief celebrant of the Mass was a pastor who had only weeks before been warned by a death squad that it was going to assassinate him. Yet Monsignor Rivera was walking around the streets without any protection and celebrating this day with his community, an event that would be interpreted by many as subversive. Nearby me, in a small alcove next to the high altar, stood the tomb of another martyr, Monsignor Romero.

Here, in this place, where so much had happened, there was an almost overpowering feeling that Jesus Christ was present with us. It was here that Oscar Romero preached his famous homilies; against the walls of this building the security forces had hurled their bombs to intimidate the people, and it was into this cathedral that thousands of terrified people rushed during Monsignor Romero's funeral when the national guard opened fire on them.

Kneeling in prayer, feeling all of this history around me, seeing the unfolding of the life, death and resurrection of Jesus before me, the rusting iron stanchions, the corrugated sheets and the distorting speakers took on a new meaning. Ugliness faded into beauty. Even the man-made bricks and mortar in this place were deeply symbolic of the journey of these people.

A short stroll from the metropolitan cathedral is the Plaza Libertad. On this morning it was crowded with people and vendors, buying and selling everything from exotic foods to Rosary beads. The Plaza does not look impressive: deteriorating statues, an overabundance of concrete and few trees. I stood there attempting to visualize what this square was like on February 28, 1977.

Ten thousand people gathered in the plaza to protest against the fraudulent elections that had recently taken place. National guardsmen surrounded the square. On the 27th, a Sunday, as most of the people present were Christians, a young Salvadoran priest, Alfonso Navarro, organized for the Mass to be transferred from a church on the edge of the square to the middle of the plaza. An altar was quickly erected. And the ten thousand gathered around Alfonso Navarro, while armed soldiers surrounded them from the nearby rooftops. The atmosphere was tense.

During the Eucharist, Father Navarro said: 'If they kill me now, you will know who is responsible.' Then some young people from Base Christian Communities handed around a note which read: 'Finally the church is where it always should have been; with the people who are surrounded by wolves.'

At about midnight the national guard began shooting into the crowd. Thousands attempted to take cover in the church of El Rosario, standing on the edge of the plaza. The guardsmen pursued those who ran, and bombed the church with gas. Some people tried to reach a neighbouring plaza but were captured and taken off to prison.

The floor of the Plaza Libertad was littered with bodies. Heavy trucks came and the dead were shovelled up. Water cannons then moved through the square hosing away the blood.

The massacre in the Plaza Libertad will not be forgotten by the people, nor will they forget that before their crucifixion they partook in the breaking of the bread and the drinking from the cup. The church had been with the people during this important chapter of their struggle.

Salvadorans remember, too, the small chapel beside La Divina Providencia Hospital where Oscar Romero was celebrating the Eucharist on the evening of March 24, 1980. As the assassins were making their way through the hospital grounds, the archbishop was concluding his homily with these words: 'This Holy Mass, this Eucharist, is clearly an act of faith. Our Christian faith shows us that in this moment contention is changed into the body of the Lord who offers himself for the redemption of the world. In this chalice, the wine is transformed into the blood that is the price of salvation. May this body broken and this blood shed for human beings encourage us to give up our body and blood to suffering and pain, as Christ did — not for self, but to bring justice and peace to our people.'

As he stood there the death squad walked up the aisle of the chapel and murdered Oscar Romero. He fell backwards and collapsed behind the altar, and lay at the feet of the giant crucifix.

I stood by that altar with the nun who had been at Romero's last supper. Forgetting the assassins, she had run to the aid of her beloved bishop. But already his God had taken him to paradise.

My time in El Salvador has been spent in many places that even my colleagues had great fear in going to.

There was one place where they refused to go. For more than five years the town of Aguilares had been a military zone. And it had remained so, not because of the civil war but as a result of a Catholic community's faith in a God of love and justice.

It had once been a serfdom where sugar barons repressed the ignorant peasant people. A group of Jesuits were sent there to establish organised parishes.

One of the pastors was Father Rutilio Grande. He was a priest who had for ten years of his ordained life stumbled in the dark and doubted his own faith and effectiveness. Then he had faced the poverty of Salvador and been converted.

At Aguilares this remarkable man set up, not traditional parishes, but a series of Base Christian Communities. He discovered that his parishioners were little more than baptised pagans who accepted the fatalism of their situation. They viewed God as they did the national guard, an authoritarian to be obeyed out of fear.

Gradually these 37 Base Christian Communities began to discover the liberating Christ. They became people of faith, hope and love rather than people of doom.

'God is not somewhere up there in the clouds sleeping in a hammock,' Rutilio Grande once told his people. 'God is here with us, building a Kingdom here on earth.'

The poor loved him and encouraged him. The rich sugar barons cursed him and plotted with the military against him.

Rutilio ignored threats to silence him. His voice continued to be heard defending the poor.

'The enslaved masses of our people, those by the side of the road, live in a feudal system six centuries old. They own neither their own land nor their lives,' said Father Rutilio.

As dusk drew in on March 12, 1977 Father Rutilio, an old man, a youth and three small boys were driving to Mass along a lonely road between Aguilares and El Paisnal.

They did not notice the vehicle tailing them.

As the death squad drew abreast with the priest's vehicle, a volley of automatic rifle fire bit into the canvas of his jeep. The death squad continued to pump bullets into the vehicle. The bodies of the priest and two of his companions were torn to pieces. Only the three small boys escaped. They fled in terror across the open fields.

A cautious, conservative archbishop drove to Aguilares to identify the bodies of his people. He gazed down on the bloodied body of the priest whom he had warned to slow down. The prelate was deeply moved. From that event and the massacre in the Plaza Libertad, Oscar Romero began to discover the suffering face of Jesus Christ. Romero too was undergoing a conversion. He was preparing to walk to the altar in La Divina Providencia.

Did peace return to this community after the assassination of the Jesuit and his friends?

Neither the faith of the people nor the hatred of the authorities abated.

They came. They came in trains. They came in trucks and landed in parachutes. Angry beasts dressed in military uniforms surrounded the Aguilares community. Those people who owned Bibles and parish hymn books were arrrested and beaten. The remaining priests were seized. Some were expelled to Guatemala; others were strung up on prison bars and tortured in front of the people.

The village was attacked and plundered. Even Rutilio's church building did not escape.

The final act of desecration was to attack the church on four sides, tearing open the Tabernacle and trampling the Blessed Sacrament into the ground.

I have seen the magestic Niagara Falls. I have seen the Andes covered in snow, and been where the great Amazon meets the Rio Silomos and the Rio Negros. But the places that I shall never forget are the metropolitan cathedral, the chapel at La Divina Provendicia Hospital, the Plaza Libertad and the story of Aguilares.

I'm quite aware that very soon the Bible and the Gospel won't be allowed to cross our borders. We'll get only the bindings, because all the pages are subversive. If Jesus himself came across the border at Chalatanago, they wouldn't let him in.

It is dangerous to be a Christian in our world. It is almost illegal to be a Catholic in our world, where the very preaching of the Gospel is subversive and where priests are exiled for preaching it.
— **Rutilio Grande.**

San Jose de la Montana Seminary in San Salvador is the major seminary in El Salvador. It has been the scene of much of the nation's recent history.

CHAPTER X

EL SALVADOR

Do Not Be Afraid

The auxiliary bishop of San Salvador, Gregorio Rosa Chavez, once asked his congregation: 'What would Isaiah have said if he had spent the last week in our country?'. The bishop went on to read all the killings, disappearances and other abuses that had occurred that week in El Salvador.

Maybe the Old Testament prophet would have denounced this injustice in a new song of the suffering servant.

I believe that if Isaiah came to El Salvador he would say to these people 'The word of God has already proclaimed the message of liberation to you who are repressed, who suffer and who cry out in pain.

'Do not be afraid my people of El Salvador,
I have saved you.
I have called you by your name,
you are mine.
If you should be dragged from your homes, and tortured in prison,
I will be with you.
And if they burn and bomb your communities,
the forces of evil will not triumph.
For I am your God —
the liberator of the poor,
I am El Salvador.'

I have visited Salvador on three occasions. Each time I am renewed in my own faith. I see the Gospel of the Liberating

Christ everywhere I go. I meet Christ's disciples going out to proclaim salvation. I witness powerless love and peace that challenges the law — the law that no longer protects God's children, but instead, exploits, rapes and plunders the dignity of these children.

I see some church leaders crossing the road and ignoring the tortured and bleeding in case they implicate themselves in this struggle.

I hear about sons and daughters who have left their father's house to seek new horizons. They are confronted by a system of sin and finally return home asking forgiveness and to be made a servant in their father's home.

And I see lots of bent figures, bodies scourged, laden down with wooden crosses.

Each visit to El Salvador takes me back to the people sheltering at San Jose de la Montana seminary. As I make my way into this place, with its high fence, its caged people, and concentration-camp-like appearance, the words of Isaiah pound in my head — 'Do not be afraid. I am with you. I have called you by your name, you are Mine'.

These are moving, marvellous and meaningful lines for the Christian who is attempting to link Biblical concepts with the plight of the suffering souls in Central America.

Passing through those gates and around the track that leads to the grounds behind the seminary I begin to see it all over again. The numbers of people are just as large. I begin to feel anger build up inside me. And I have to stop myself yelling out at the top of my voice; 'My God — where are you? How much more can these little people take? Why do you abandon them so?'.

Then I sit down with them and listen to their stories.

As they speak, my anger dies. Their faces, their stories, their fresh exhilarating faith take you deeper into the words of Isaiah.

Yes, they are afraid. They're so terrified that they tremble as they speak. But in spite of their fear they have a knowledge that they are walking through hell with a Saviour who will not fail, will not be crushed, will not be bought off for material gain, who loves them and holds them tightly, a Saviour who calls each one precious and knows every name.

Despite all the fear, they are prepared to free themselves and walk alongside that Saviour.

They are not afraid to let go.

I realise that these people know Christ so much better than I because I am still a novice in the process of conversion.

'We were only Christians and we used to attend Christian services,' the mother told me.

I had brought Dina, my World Vision colleague from Guatemala, with me. She was my interpreter.

'We used to go to Bible studies conducted by our priest. Because we were part of that church, the national guard came and murdered my husband.'

The woman recalled how her husband tried to run when he saw the soldiers. 'But they killed him. They killed the Catholic priest too.'

This woman was putting new power into the words of Isaiah.

'We trust in God. Believing in God is not a crime. We know that God will do justice to us because all this is unfair and unjust.'

Lencho, too, spoke with Dina in Spanish.

'I worked with the priests and I was accused. When the priests came to do their spiritual work in our village, I helped them. I was regarded by the army as a subversive.'

Then one day Lencho was working in the fields when he saw the soldiers approaching. He knew they were looking for him. He attracted their attention and then ran into the forest, believing that the squad would pursue him. But they did not.

'Instead they raided my house and killed my family. The village was raided because it was Catholic,' said Lencho.

Maria was a catechist in a rural town.

One day the national guard and members of the death squad, ORDEN, came to her town.

'We were sleeping when they arrived. They broke in and took my husband and son outside. They were tied up and beaten with rifles. They were then taken away and decapitated,' said Maria.

A grandmother, Elisa, told me about the barbaric raid that reduced her Base Christian Community to rubble.

'There is nothing left there now,' she said.

Without hesitation she recalled the events that had forced her to run. Providing this kind of information to the wrong person would mean certain death for her. But within these walls, there was trust and a certain boldness. These people believed that despite the enemy that lurked around this property, those within were friends.

'The area around our village was attacked for 22 days. It was attacked from the air and the ground,' Elisa told me. She said that each time she hears an aeroplane now she trembles.

'I remember what they did to our village. My two sons were killed in the bombardments.'

What chance did these people have when the Salvadoran air force flew over their flimsy village with the most sophisticated machines of death that the United States could provide?

But the bombs falling from the sky were not the most horrific instance in that village. When the planes stopped their bombing, the soldiers surrounded the smouldering ruins and charged in for their final spoils.

Let me record these events, not to expose violence for violence's sake, but so that the truth of Central America can be told as reflected through the voiceless Salvadoran people. Let me remind you this was not a guerilla camp, but a community of Christians.'

The soldiers accused the villagers of being guerillas. During the questioning, the soldiers would take a victim and cut off part of a finger. Then they would cut away more and more.

Elisa recalled the insane bloodbath that followed. The soldiers must have gone crazy.

'They blindfolded people. They attacked people with machetes. Pregnant women were cut open. Children were decapitated. I saw them throw heads one way and bodies another,' said Elisa.

In contrast with these memories of death is the resurrection that one can see at San Jose de la Montana. Those who live here are from many areas. They come as terrified strangers.

They come mainly from Base Christian Communities. They come with simple faith, yet astonishing faith. Therefore it is not surprising to see these Christians rebuilding their community, in this small enclosure surrounded by walls.

A large lean-to building serves as the community kitchen. Women in white aprons boil rice, bake tortillas, prepare soup. In their midst was a small smiling-faced man, decked out in a chef's hat.

I asked Juan if he was a chef by trade. No, he replied, his job was preaching the Word in village communities where there was a shortage of priests. He instructed the children, preparing them for reconciliation, communion, and confirmation.

The national guard had been instructed to flush out these lay instructors. Catechists could disappear or be killed without attracting the same attention as a priest or nun.

Information about Juan was passed on to these soldiers. The catechist was apprehended and taken in for questioning. He was warned to stop this dangerous activity.

Then he was abducted a second time.

He was subjected to torture.

As he spoke, the words of Rutilio Grande came back to me.

'Very soon the Bible and the Gospel won't be allowed to cross our borders.

'We'll get only the bindings, because the pages are subversive.

'It is almost illegal to be a Catholic in our world.'

This is what Father Grande meant: 'Illegal to be a Catholic — illegal to be a Christian.'

Juan's fingers were horribly deformed. The soldiers had bound his two thumbs tightly together.

'The thumbs swelled up badly,' said Juan. 'After 15 days the national guard pulled off the cord and all the flesh came away too.'

They bound Juan's ankles too. They threw him to the ground and these thugs trampled his stomach into the floor.

'For a year afterwards, I thought all my insides were destroyed.'

His family fled. He is now trying to locate them.

So Juan is now a cook in the camp?

'No,' corrected this beautiful person, 'I am still a catechist.'

What does all this do to an Australian, a Christian, a World Vision worker, who lives in complete comfort and safety? It does not destroy, it uplifts, particularly when the camp director calls to you that there is somebody else who is waiting to see you again.

I had often wondered about the 12-year-old boy I had met a year earlier at this seminary.

Domingo's body was still badly disfigured. Hair had started to grow over the hideous wounds on his scalp, but the wounds inflicted by machetes were still very visible.

The boy was not sitting in a corner brooding. He was too busy. Domingo was making hammocks, which the archdiocese of San Salvador was selling for him. He could still smile and talk about his future.

'I would like, one day, to go back to my town and become a farmer like my father.'

He so much reflected the Salvadoran people. All the death and suffering did not preclude a future, a future that required reform.

How I hope that Domingo will be allowed to go home and take up the vision that his father had, the vision that was so ruthlessly interrupted.

On my third visit to San Jose de la Montana, Domingo had gone.

Maybe he had returned to his old community. Maybe he was apprehended immediately he passed through the seminary gates and onto the street. Maybe the repressive system would force his struggle in a different direction, into the hills to fight a bloody war.

A mother related her experience to Dina in Spanish. It had been a long day. Dina had listened to so much tragedy then attempted to put it into English in the best way she could.

The woman was still speaking, but Dina was no longer listening. The World Vision woman had broken down in uncontrollable tears.

'I can't do this anymore. I can't, ' she cried. Dina's voice was drowning out the mother next to her.

'This woman has finished me,' sobbed Dina.

After some time Dina calmed down a little and translated the previous conversation.

The woman had told Dina that the soldiers had shot the people and had chased many away. As these troops went through the village they grabbed the children, some only two and three years old, and hanged them from the verandahs.

This was not new to Dina. She had lived in Guatemala. One night, she had told me what happened to her people when they stood up against the system. Why then had this experience in Salvador affected her so greatly?

I believe, like so many of us, Dina did not want to believe it. Attempting to exist in this brutality, many people, Christians included, who have responsible positions in these societies want to convince themselves that it could not happen. If it does go on, then it only affects committed Communists who are undermining the system of the country.

But Dina was again confronting reality. A new country, new victims. The same sin.

We are all similar. It is easy to neglect the root evils of the Salvadors, the Lebanons, the Ugandas and the Australias. They are political issues. These are often thought to be the issues of the world, and it's easier to say that Christians must immerse themselves into the spiritual dimension of the Gospel.

But Christ is up to his neck in the things of the world.

Do not be afraid,
for I have saved you.
I have called you by your name,
you are mine.
Should you pass through the sea,
I will be with you,
all through rivers,
they will not swallow you up.
Should you walk through fire,
you will not be scorched
the flames will not burn you.
For I am Yahweh, your God,
the Holy One of Israel, your Saviour.
— Isaiah 43: 1-3.

San Francisco camp, Chile. A human jungle, where the people are oppressed by a military regime, manipulated by crime networks and exploited by each other. San Francisco is not without hope. People are starting to believe in themselves; discovering trust in one another; building communities.

CHAPTER XI

The Cardinal and the General

Chile conjures up certain images in my mind: the military coup exploding onto streets of chaos. News footage of the armed forces bombing the presidential palace. A football stadium with terrified souls caged like animals on its arena and tormented screams from the bowels of its grandstands. Security forces purging all who had, or were suspected of having, another opinion.

When I arrived there in February, 1987, that Chile had gone.

There I was in the magnificent capital, Santiago, in the peak of summer. Side by side stood the grandeur of colonial times and modern day steel and glass spiralling up into the skies. The streets were clean and bustling with people. The underground rail system was a safe mode of transport, without a single disfigurement of graffiti.

People were out buying, eating in the profusion of quaint Spanish restaurants. The ceremonial guard at the beautifully restored presidential palace appeared not to notice the tourists trespassing on to the official lawns to photograph this landmark.

The national congress building was the first hint that everything was not normal.

This seat of Chilean government edged by well-kept gardens is a mausoleum, a place of memories, of freedom stopped and destroyed.

The pride of this South American republic, a history of democracy, was lost in the ruthless coup of 1973.

Along the Pacific coast the nation was at play — packed onto the wide strips of sand at the popular resorts like San Antonio and Vina del Mar.

There appeared to be no repression and poverty did not seem to be excessive. No wonder tourists and business people responded in such favourable terms. Chile is seen as progressive, alive and full of Latin charm.

This could be southern Europe.

A week before I arrived, a prominent TV evangelist from the United States had given his blessing to Chile, its economic development and most of all its leader, Augusto Pinochet.

The danger of visiting Chile is that you can easily become lost in the glossy exterior. I think the TV evangelist might have been overcome by the military strongman's intoxicating potion.

Break through the veneer and you are left wandering in an abyss. Like the Congress building, everything is empty. A skilfully and professionally cultivated exterior disguises the facts of a brutal military dictator and a state run by the national security service rather than the will of the people.

The guns and the torture chambers are almost silent now. The trade unions, the student organisations, the popular peoples' groups and the opposition parties are dead, exiled or so badly bruised and battered that they rarely muster the energy to protest.

The middle class live with an uneasy peace, wondering when it will be interrupted. When pressed on political questions they temper their reply with, 'We dare not think about the chaos that might have befallen the nation if the military had not stepped in'.

If you are persistent then you will finally crash through the veneer and find yourself in the genuine Chile.

San Francisco is an illegal squatters' town on the edge of Santiago. Taxis refuse to take your fare if you name it as your destination. Buses terminate a long way away. It is the home of 11,000 people, migrants from provincial cities and rural villages. Many are *desperados* — reduced to despair by the circumstances in which they live. Some have reluctantly adopted crime as a means of survival. Others are frightened women, alone, stripped of their last ounce of dignity.

Camp St Francis is a maze of people, flies, dilapidated dwellings and violence. This seething mass of broken human beings and junk is devoid of basic services like schools, electricity and sanitation.

Everybody is poor, frustrated and angry. The settlement does not reflect the courage or the inspiration of your Brazilian or Salvadoran Christian Base Communities. St Francis is a jungle — exacerbated by a regime that treats the poor with contempt.

For a nation so entrenched in the doctrine of national security, there is an amazing lack of national security for the Chilean people.

While the poor in most Third World countries are subjected to government neglect, in Chile the little people are all but abandoned. This is particularly highlighted in times of disaster.

During the serious flooding in 1987, when many Chilean shanties collapsed, General Pinochet was asked what emergency aid would be provided by the government. The general replied: 'Faith and patience, no more'.

Since the military coup in 1973, thousands of people have fled to the cities in search of work. The mushrooming of the slum districts has compounded the health problems. Yet during this period, the regime has cut public health spending by about 30%.

Major axing has occurred too in public works spending and employment in the public sector.

I have never been to a shanty town totally bereft of hope, and San Francisco is no different. There in the grime and the lawlessness, ordinary people cry out for love and compassion. Here is where the truth of Chile is exposed before you. Pleasantries like, 'The poor are always good', are shattered. Down in St Francis' camp conditions have made some of the poor bad. They exploit and harass one another. The powerful poor prey on the powerless poor. After the police and the crime mongers have been through this place, frustration becomes hostility and the poor strike out against one another.

I was in a small feeding and medical centre in the heart of San Francisco, jointly run by World Vision and two St Vincent de Paul nuns. I was told that this was as close as I could get to the inmates of this camp.

Our vehicle had bravely entered these environs. Once behind the flimsy gates of the centre, I was escorted into a clean but shabby feeding shelter.

Some of the leaders at San Francisco had approached the St Vincent de Paul order inviting the sisters to come and establish a school. Each week thousands of children were spending many idle hours with only the lure of drugs and vice to break the monotony.

Two nuns came. However, the authorities refused them permission to open a school. The regime classified San Francisco as an illegal human camp. Schools encouraged a permanency in places like this. Despite the ruling, the sisters stayed. They quickly discovered more than crime and filth. They saw seriously malnourished babies. All around them, women abandoned by their menfolk attempted to feed their children. These were frightened women, often forced into casual relationships in the hope of having some man around to protect them and their youngsters.

Nuns can be tough. Refused permission to open a school, these two religious women got to and started a health clinic. They approached World Vision to help provide food and medical assistance.

'We began with 13 babies on the first day. Now we have 212 babies in our care. The number increases every day,' said one of the nuns, Sister Alissia. 'A survey was taken. There are 5901 children in this camp. Here we are, just a grain of sand.'

But they are a grain of sand that the camp could not do without.

They had lost the first round with the authorities, but not the second. A team of mothers came to the centre each day. The nuns encouraged them to help prepare the meals for the children, participate in sewing classes, set up a community bakery and clean the centre. To prevent this being a simple handout centre, the nuns applied to the authorities to pay the women for this work. The request was granted. The women are receiving benefits under the government's 'minimum employment program'. The payments are well below the minimum allowed under the labour laws of Chile. But it is a start and begins to recognise the worth of these people.

Most of the women have been abandoned by their husbands. Couples are moving in and out of relationships. While this might give some sense of protection, it offers nothing in the way of stability for the family. Nor does it do anything to help restore a woman's dignity. Male drunkenness and violence are common. There is no point in calling on the police to rescue mother and children from domestic violence. The family must suffer in silence.

Both sisters understand the reality of Latin society. Rather than moralising about these relationships, they busy themselves trying to re-establish the dignity that has been beaten out of the shanty-town women.

Nobody is safe in this camp. Gangs roam its streets, mugging and raping. Some of the thugs have threatened to rob the nuns. Crazy Richard, one of the gang leaders, forbade any of his hoodlums to harm the two sisters. The nuns believe however that he was motivated by religious superstition. He had a very deep devotion to the Virgin of Montserrat. He somehow connected her powers with the nuns. Recently Richard was gunned down. The gang carried his corpse on the top of the coffin through the streets of the camp. As the funeral procession moved along, the gang was busily pick-pocketing the bystanders.

Another leader, known as The Guts, told Sister Alissia that it was impossible for him to change. He had already killed three people and he knew that he would go the same way. A short time later, they found him dead. Somebody had cut his throat.

Within the tiny shacks, the sisters have discovered that there is not even a basic understanding of hygiene.

'There is no understanding about cleaning pots and pans. Sometimes these pots and pans are dirtier than the ones used by the dogs in the camp,' explained Sister Alissia.

But the struggle to teach mothers and build community goes on. While the visitor has only admiration for this development among the poor, the reality is that in the eyes of the government, the nuns are engaged in an illegal ministry. However the Archbishop of Santiago, Cardinal Fresno, has gone to celebrate the Mass at San Francisco. His presence in a place like this is a powerful statement to the poor and the authorities. He too encourages the nuns to persist with their work.

Before I left San Francisco, the nuns did consent to allow me to walk down the narrow slum streets and meet some of the people. They warned me however that I was embarking on a dangerous assignment. They set strict conditions. I had to walk in front with a young woman from the World Vision office. The two sisters said that they would tail a few paces behind as a type of rear defence. Sounding like a pair of veterans, they explained that muggers generally attacked from behind. So off we went in this ridiculous procession, the two visitors to San Francisco cautiously walking out in front while a couple of nuns followed behind protecting us from sudden assault by a mob of thugs. I did say earlier that nuns can be tough. Maybe the thugs believe that too. I'm sure that God must have gazed down and smiled to himself. As I walked along I encountered only friendly greetings from mothers who came out from behind the walls of their shacks to speak with the nuns — ordinary human beings wanting help, friendship and somebody they could trust. But as we returned to the centre there was sudden movement and I was mobbed by about 20 children, their little brown faces full of love.

Thank God for the two women in white. Maybe there was a chance that these loving youngsters would not be transformed into somebody else — hard, bitter and angry.

San Francisco is not a unique chapter in Pinochet's Chile. There are similar shanty towns all round the big cities.

On the other side of the capital, I met another community of squatters. For twenty years they have lived under crowded and violent conditions. This is a notorious drug distribution centre. With mass unemployment and no government services, the poor have little choice. They have fallen easy prey to the powerful crime syndicates. People slouch around street corners, openly carrying small plastic bags of drugs. Cars roll in with cocaine and marijuana for the peddlers' own supply, and enough for them to sell so that their families may live. Even the teenagers are agents for the stuff.

A Protestant pastor, whose church is in the middle of the slum, told me about children of seven and eight hooked on drugs.

Prostitution too is rampant. Customers cruise in in their big cars from the rich quarters of Santiago, usually picking up the youngest girls. If the rich are not after sex, then they are chasing their supply of cocaine.

The pastor told me that little is being done to rehabilitate these people or provide alternative industries so that they can support their families. The pastor had asked the government to help him build a centre so that a rehabilitation program could begin. But like the nuns, he was refused all assistance.

Yet you never leave the presence of the poor without learning something. A woman told me that she lived with three other abandoned mothers and their children. Their home comprised two small bedrooms, a sitting room and a tiny kitchen. I asked her how she coped with the problems of overcrowding. Without a pause she replied — 'You don't have many problems because you\have to learn to share with people. You have to know how to live here. People do share together.'

In other parts of Santiago the poor have recognised the need to unify as a community and begin the process of reform.

An Australian Columban priest, who has worked and lived among the slum dwellers for eight years, was blunt when he said: 'No miracles are worked here. It's a struggle and it's frustrating. There are no heroes. All we do is to attempt to keep alive the faith and a hope for the future'.

He serves his people the best way he can, and reminded me that parishes here were not like the ones at home. In the urban areas it is not unusual to pastor to between 40,000 and 80,000 people.

However, he proudly spoke about a community of fishermen,

who could not attend Sunday Mass so they grouped together and arranged a prayer time on Monday. About mothers, undergoing a two year training course in preparation for their children's first communion.

'This group has studied, prayed and shared together. Hopefully they will stay together as a community group', the priest told me with a sound of optimism in his voice. The priest was excited because the leadership in these shanty-town parishes is being assumed by the laity. The downtrodden are discovering that they have a vocation as proclaimers of the good news.

And if the community impact seems to outsiders as less than spectacular compared to other Latin countries, the Chilean regime sees it as serious business. The awakening of the poor by meddling clerics puts the security forces on the alert. A number of priests have been arrested and beaten. Some foreign clergy have been expelled. But the Pinochet machine handles the church carefully. After 15 years of assault on all forms of opposition, the church is the only dissenting survivor. The general has destroyed and divided all his opposition, only God's church remains.

The church has endured because it is too big and too influential and the regime too clever to declare war on the Body of Christ.

To appreciate the relationship between Church and State one has to understand two important historical facts about Chile.

First, during its post-colonial history, Chile has generally enjoyed democracy. Only twice have the troops left their barracks and seized power — in 1931 and 1973.

Second, the Catholic Church was equipped to handle the genocide that was suddenly waged against its people. Prominent Jesuit, Father Renato Poblette, says the church carries fewer noticeable scars than its sisters in Central America.

'This has happened because the government has respect for the church. The regime quickly realised that the Catholic Church was conscientised'.

And maybe some of this respect was born out of the knowledge that the church was too powerful and that the Christian faith has a long history of growth during times of persecution. Therefore, it is smarter to let loose the secret police and the death squads on the organised left and try to ignore the institutional church. Certainly, during the early days of the dictatorship, three priests were murdered. But unlike other Latin countries, the Chilean church has had a long experience and understanding of being the church of the poor and living justly.

Renato Poblette was one of the authors of the Medellin and Puebla papers used by Latin bishops at both of these famous conferences.

'The Chilean church was very advanced at the time of Medellin. Chileans were practising most of the issues raised at Medellin, regarding social justice, five years earlier.

'Today you see some differences in thinking between bishops, nevertheless on issues of human rights and justice, all are on the same line', said Father Poblette.

Much of the respect gained by the church centres around the former Archbishop of Santiago, Raul Cardinal Silva Henriquez. This courageous leader confronted the regime, denouncing its evil oppression. The military was able to divide and destroy every institution in that country with the exception of Cardinal Silva's church.

He gave refuge to displaced people. He opened a peace committee right under the noses of this national security regime.

When General Pinochet finally ordered its closure, condemning it as a subversive Communist front, Cardinal Silva re-established the committee, not as an inter-church peace committee but rather as an official Vicariate of Solidarity, placing it under the direct authority of his archdioceses in Santiago. It was a stroke of genius. How could the regime order the closure of a official organisation under the direction of the Cardinal Archbishop, without running headlong into the most respected body in Chile? The general was not prepared to let himself fall into that type of trap.

'My experience in the first meetings between Cardinal Silva and General Pinochet was that we obtained many things', said Father Poblette.

But these private consultations put the church in a difficult position. On one hand the Cardinal knew that he was dealing with a military dictatorship. The way to win a positive response was to carry out negotiations in private.

'If everything is done in private,' Father Poblette explained, 'the church appears to be silent on issues. Silence is interpreted by the people as complicity. So you have to mix your strategies.'

The Vicariate of Solidarity continues to pick up the pieces of broken people while the dictatorship stalks around its perimeter waiting an opportunity to pounce on this abomination.

All Chileans, Catholic, Protestant and non-believers, know that when they are under attack from or being abused by the state, they have someone to protect them. Today the Vicariate of Solidarity is one of the most respected legal aid centres in Latin America.

Alongside its legal office is a medical service to treat the victims who are tortured while being held in detention. Many are too frightened to seek treatment in state hospitals.

'Twice in 1986, the Vicariate doctor was jailed and one of the lawyers was detained,' the senior legal officer at the Vicariate, Roberto Garriton Merino, told me. He explained that there were two forms of repression practised in Chile.

'There is legal repression exercised through the law. The rights of a person are subjected to the will of the authorities. In other words everything is legal. The authorities are the supreme power. They make the laws. The courts are under the responsibility to make judgements on these laws.

'Then there is criminal repression: the murders of political opponents by bands supported and protected by the government.'

When I was at the Vicariate, it was no longer peak repression. However, during this lean period, the office was handling 100 new cases a week. This legal aid office confirmed that doctors too are frequently party to prison torture.

When victims are to be released from police detention the victims are examined by a doctor who certifies that the person is in good health when leaving the jail. The Vicariate has evidence that it is generally a doctor who determines if a political prisoner can endure another bashing.

The thugs in military and police uniforms even have nicknames for their obscene practices.

The barbecue is a metal bed where victims are tied and electrodes fixed to their head, hands, feet, in the mouth and on the genitals.

The telephone is when a victim's ears are violently boxed simultaneously by the torturers' fists.

The submarine is when the head is submerged into water or sometimes into a sewer. Others have their bodies twisted into distorted forms and are then left suspended in the air.

All of these tortures have been fully documented. One very reliable source told me that wild animals and reptiles had been used to torture and terrify political victims. However, while he believed this to be true, it has not been fully documented.

General Pinochet once commented on the legal aid office, 'When the Vicariate jumps up and down, the world jumps up and down'.

Thank God it does.

Food in empty stomachs will sour and wounds will fester even with the best administered medical treatment, if God's children are allowed to be paralysed and disfigured by madmen in power.

Take heed of the events that have occurred in a land proud of its freedom.

The words are found engraved on battered bodies
everywhere the warnings break the deafening silence:
Democracy is fragile.
History can change.
The disciples must never sleep — the cohort and the palace
guard are always near.
The gates of hell can snare the people of God.
But unconditional love means that the faithful will not be
abandoned.
They will be renewed to pass through the deadly corridors of
oppression.

Before me a palace was disintegrating.
A president was executed.
A nation was put into chains.
A great tradition died.
In the turmoil that erupted,
I saw a tall empty wooden cross.
And I knew that the resurrection of Chile
had already begun.
— An observer in Chile.

A Guatemalan Indian mother and son. They have been victims of the wholesale murder in their country. Almost all the victims with whom the author spoke were active members in their local parish.

CHAPTER XII

The Sacking of El Quiche

Guatemala is unforgettable.

Memories, voices, faces and experiences are indelibly marked in my mind.

The shaking hands of a bishop, as he told me how military repression had forced the closure of his diocese.

Trying to sleep in a warm bed knowing that at the doorstep of my comfortable hotel a group of boys were sleeping in a cardboard box.

Being in attendance at a conference that was suddenly called to a halt when the chairman announced that in neighbouring El Salvador the archbishop, Oscar Romero, had just been assassinated.

Being in the tiny Guatemalan village of St Anthony of the Warm Waters and hearing the church bells and the music echoing across the mountains as Indians mourned the death of Oscar Romero.

Walking to Mass early one Sunday morning along the main street in Guatemala City and seeing the barrels of rifles jutting out between sandbags waiting for another terrorist attack.

Being welcomed into the home of a slum-dweller whose shanty sat at the edge of a deep rubbish dump.

Sitting in the central square, opposite the Palicio Nacional, as a small shoe-shine boy told me how his meagre earnings helped his mother feed her children. His father was a drunkard who gave his family no support, only hidings. The boy stopped in mid-sentence, grabbed his dusters, polish and box and fled.

One of the extortionist thugs had spotted him. The boy had not paid his protection money.

A Protestant theologian summed up the reality in Guatemala when he told me; 'Nobody asks questions any more. If you want to live in peace, you shut up. If you want to live you don't get involved'.

Somebody described Guatemala as being like Nazi Germany. The system inculcates so much fear that nobody dares to notice what is going on. Even Christians who believe in love and service of one's neighbour were not inclined to enquire what was occurring around the corner. Friends were uncomfortable when I asked about the political situation. They were happy to talk about the poor and the band-aid that was being distributed in the name of Christ to relieve suffering. But if the question arose — 'what is being done to defend the rights of the weak?', most people would respond with a blank stare and a silent shrug.

A World Vision colleague had confronted me once with the statement: 'You don't live here. You can never start to imagine what they do to people in Guatemala who ask questions'.

The sophisticated communications machine in Guatemala makes the security in neighbouring Central American states look futile.

A priest, exiled from Guatemala, commented to me that one could get back into most Latin countries and be working for some weeks before the authorities became aware of their presence. In Guatemala an exile would be picked up within hours. I could understand the nervousness of the people who just wanted to live.

Each time I visited Guatemala, my friends would shake their heads and say: 'It's worse'.

In 1980, the year of my first visit, military dictator Lukas Garcia was in power — a brutal man, who commanded an extremely efficient and destructive army and security network. Garcia's repression so embarrassed the President of the United States that Jimmy Carter finally banned all military aid to this regime.

But Guatemala was one of the few Latin nations that could

step aside from the stars and bars, remain rigidly opposed to the hammer and sickle, and survive. Church people reminded me that Guatemala had other influential friends, for example in Israel. Banning of military aid totally failed to effect change, and Garcia continued as before.

However, not everybody chose to be silent about what was going on in that country.

Monsignor Jose Ramiro Pellecer, a deeply Christian man, not only concerned himself with the spiritual welfare of his people, but publicly demanded respect for their human rights.

He had identified one urgent problem in a maze of problems plaguing Guatemala. Bishop Pellecer saw how the powers of violence and repression were using the profound divisions that ruptured the Body of Christ. He spoke to me of a dream which was about to come true. He was bringing together Catholics and Protestant clergy and lay people.

'We have talked about if for four years and following this Pentecost Sunday we will be meeting together,' smiled the bishop.

Guatemala has one of the largest Protestant populations in Latin America. The majority of Protestants were fundamentalist products of equally fundamentalist missionaries from the United States.

Monsignor Pellecer was an island whipped by heavy seas on all sides. Some claimed he was not radical enough. Others saw him as a subversive and had threatened his life. He was scorned by many evangelicals because he was a Catholic and already he was being labelled a Protestant bishop by some of his own flock.

Pentecost came and Catholic seminary doors were thrown open to Protestants to come in and meet the young priests in training.

There was prayer, dialogue and worship.

At the end of the week many were amazed at what they shared in common. However, most were not yet prepared to admit it.

The next time I met Bishop Pellecer, the death toll of priests in Guatemala had risen to double figures. There was also an escalation in the death toll of catechists and other lay religious leaders. So many laity had died or disappeared that it was no longer possible for church officials to keep an accurate count.

Jose Pellecer had recently received news about one of his close brothers, Father Carlos Alberto Galvez, murdered by a goon squad in the town of Chimaitenango.

Always a poor and oppressed Mayan community, Chimaitenango was now a terrorised town. I went there, against the wishes of my colleagues, and saw what the guerillas had done to public buildings. I also heard what the military and the police had done to the people.

When a friend heard that I had gone there and taken a woman from World Vision as my guide he was amazed and somewhat annoyed.

'You know what happens to people at roadblocks in that region. I don't have to tell you what they do to women out there,' said my friend.

Father Carlos Galvez had stepped out of his church after a baptismal service. The church was on the edge of the city square. It was market day and the square was crowded. As he walked down the steps of the church, gunmen appeared out of the crowd and shot him. No investigation was carried out into the priest's death.

'I studied with Carlos. He was my brother in Christ. He knew his parish well and the people knew him. He was murdered because he identified with his people,' Monsignor Pellecer told me.

Father Carlos came under observation after he spoke to army officials about compulsory military training on Sunday mornings for members of his parish.

'Why do 100 men have to spend so much money travelling down to the city on Sunday mornings,' the priest asked the commanding officer, 'when you could send up one officer to the village to train them?'

'He spoke on behalf of peasants asking for decent wages so that they could take care of their families. He spoke about the lack of health services that they gave to the poor,' explained the bishop.

Father Carlos had also asked a rich landowner to share his fresh water spring with the poor people. After long discussions, the landowner allowed the peasants to use his spring. However, Carlos Galvez was asking too much. His voice had become too loud and his proclamation of the Gospel had begun threatening too many.

The whole town turned out for his funeral — a visible witness that his death was not in vain.

The voice of Christ's disciples was not restricted to one rural town.

In the capital, President Lukas Garcia had had enough of clergy who no longer sat peacefully in their confessionals. He used a terrorist bombing incident that shook the Palacio Nacional, to issue a blunt warning to the guerillas and to that section of the church which had been outspoken on issues of social justice.

The president chose the balcony of the damaged palace and guaranteed his audience by trucking in public servants from all sections of the city.

Lukas Garcia charged that some religions in Guatemala had dedicated themselves to indoctrinating the people.

'To those men and women (priests and nuns), we must tell you that you must devote your time to guiding souls or we will have to remove you and eliminate you from this country,' warned the president.

Garcia then called on the crowd to support him on this issue. His loyal collection of stooges reciprocated. Soon after the president's warning, Bishop Pellecer told me that if the government wanted the church to remain silent on issues of justice, and not support the poor against the oppressors, then the Catholic Church could not accomodate such a request.

But Garcia's public berating of the church was another calculated step in a much larger strategy. Bishop Pellecer spoke about a ten-year plan, drawn up by oppressive interests to destroy the Catholic Church. While never recognised as radical, the Guatemalan Church already exercised an influence that was unnerving the ruling elite. The plan was already under way, with the state employing squads to exterminate active members of the laity and the clergy.

Tempting inducements were offered to fundamentalist Protestants who perceived evangelist opportunities to reform
what they saw as a superstitious and dominant church. And so
they justified their acceptance of these dubious handouts.
Money, entry visas, and land were seen as necessary to
enhance their soul-winning ministry for Christ.

These fundamentalist groups were not only accusing the
Catholic Church in Guatemala of being neo-Christians, but also
of being agents of the forces of the violent left. The division ran
even deeper. Many Catholics had linked themselves with the
hard-line right of the church which gave lip service to the
needs of the poor but active support to those who went on
stifling the progressive church of the oppressed. There were
also an ever-growing number of disillusioned Catholics who
saw too many of their prelates and clergy as pawns of the
system.

Church reforms were too few and introduced too late.

The intelligence network not only penetrated the Christian
Base Communities in the villages and cities, but also weaved
its way into the very heart of the church bureaucracy. Information was quickly passed back to the authorities about the
actions of certain church dignitaries. But Jose Pellecer smiled
when the subject of church spies was raised.

'They are doing their jobs. They are hard working, these
spies. We get to know the spies and after a time we are able to
learn about the things that the government is up to, too.'

Both the government and the church remain powerful insti-
tutions in Guatemala, explained the bishop.

'The government exerts its power through guns, but the
church must trust in the Holy Saviour for its power,' said
Bishop Pellecer.

He admitted that the church still had a long way to go if it
was to be an effective servant of the poor.

'Guatemala needs grace, salvation and conversion. Our trust
is too much in the police, the army, the judges and money. God
is telling us we are putting our trust in the wrong things. He is
saying trust in Me instead of other things.'

After the eventual overthrow of Lukas Garcia, Guatemala had a Protestant thrust into the presidential palace: a change from a long line of brutal military despots claiming allegiance to the Catholic faith, but nevertheless a tyrant who used the army and para-military thugs to commit wholesale genocide in Indian villages.

President Rios Montt became the champion of the fundamentalist sects, who saw him as a saviour. The dictator thrilled his supporters with his vigorous proclamation of his born-again experience and his solemn pledge to crush the backbone of the Communist guerilla movements.

In the rural areas his scorched earth policy destroyed almost everything but the spirit of those dedicated to liberation.

I had once questioned a senior general in the Garcia regime about the infamous reputation his country had in regard to human rights, and if it worried him.

Yes, he did admit that there were human rights abuses from the army and the guerillas.

'There is injustice in this country,' replied the military leader, 'but it is just as real in the US and in other Western nations, particularly in relation to trade.'

He used bananas as an example. At one time, Guatemala could sell five boxes of bananas for one drum of imported oil. Today more than 10 boxes of bananas did not buy even one drum of oil.

'Human rights begin with the economy,' declared the general. He went on to make his point: 'The West sets the conditions when it comes to exporting Guatemalan bananas, but to import a Japanese motor car or a Swiss watch, it is the exporter who has all the say.'

During my visit to Guatemala in 1984 a meeting was set up for me with the director of Caritas, the local Catholic relief and development agency. As I entered the Director's office, a man was leaving. During discussions about the needs and aspirations of the poor, I questioned the Caritas director about Juan Gerardi, the Bishop of El Quiche, who had been forced to shut down his diocese because so many of his people were being assassinated. On his return from a visit to Rome, the authorities had refused to allow him back into the country. I was interested to know whether the exiled bishop was still in Costa Rica.

The Caritas official smiled. The bishop had quietly re-entered Guatemala but had not been able to return to El Quiche. The aid official enquired whether I would be interested in speaking with Juan Gerardi. He then told me that the man who had walked out of his office as I was entering, was the Bishop of El Quiche.

A few moments later Monsignor Gerardi was being ushered back into the Caritas office.

The bishop was very different to the way I had pictured him. His face was very drawn, and a deathly grey colour. He sat down at the desk and waited for me to speak. His expression did not change. There was no smile. I noticed that his hands were continually shaking. He appeared very tense. Juan Gerardi appeared at first glance to lack the charisma of other Latin bishops whom I had met. But maybe none whom I had met had suffered like this man.

El Quiche was infrequently spoken about. Nobody I knew dared to go there. This Indian province was a grotesque battle field that the people in Guatemala City wanted to forget.

Sitting before me was the man, the shepherd, whose sheep had been led to the slaughter, and he had borne their suffering. He was a simple country bishop who was taken by force and finally expelled and separated from his people, while the world remained silent.

I was now looking deeper at the ashen face that showed no expression of emotion.

Bishop Gerardi had not long returned to his homeland after three years of exile. He was hesitant in his speech. He avoided my questions which was completely understandable. I was a stranger who had blown in off the street. He was a wanted man. I was experiencing the direct result of the successful state terror machine. He could trust few people. Even my being a fellow Christian was no guarantee of reliability. As we passed time with guarded conversation, I gradually penetrated the rigid exterior and started to feel a warmth from the man sitting

104

opposite. Uncertain smiles began to creep across the bishop's face. I sensed too, that he had broken through my exterior and maybe was discovering a hint of genuine concern for him and his people. Maybe for a moment we had been able to glance into each other's hidden soul and liked what we saw. Something happened which allowed the strained words and the distrust to fade.

Gerardi began telling me a story that shall haunt me always. I have called it the sacking of El Quiche.

The Guatemalan nation had been forced into submission by the Spanish conquistadors in the 1500s. In 1980 another army bloodied these Indian lands.

This time it was not a Spanish-commanded army of conscripted Indians from Mexico, but a Guatemalan-commanded army of conscripted Indians from Guatemala.

The sacking of El Quiche never reached the international media's front pages. The state terror machine was too effective. It was too clever to allow its repression to rebound against it. But Juan Gerardi did witness it. He saw his people murdered at random during six months of insanity. However, even he did not see the final holocaust when village after village was put to the torch under the government's official scorched earth policy. This happened because finally the effective voice of Gerardi's church had been destroyed.

In January 1980, recalled Monsignor Gerardi, the Mayan Indians became familiar with the presence of guerilla forces. Small groups of freedom fighters, as many Guatemalans call the guerillas, began creeping into villages and addressing the community. This generally occurred at night. Their speeches were short. The ideology espoused by these revolutionaries was not understood by many of the Indians. Then as quietly as they arrived, the small bands would disappear.

On their heels was the army. Aware of the guerilla presence through its network of spies, the soldiers would terrify the Indians.

Bishop Gerardi's position was very clear in this situation.

'We never supported the guerillas. We did not support the army either.'

The guerillas continued their unexpected visits, believing that their propaganda would win the support of the communities. The military's counter to these night calls was to kill the village people. There is no doubt that in this war of persuasion, the guerillas were clearly the winners.

The soldiers accused the people of supporting and feeding the rebels. They picked out community leaders as their murder victims. Nuns and catechists explained to the confused and frightened people what both sides were doing. The bishop produced a newspaper to be distributed throughout the diocese and to be read from every pulpit. It explained the events, championed the people's human rights and condemned the violence.

Juan Gerardi spoke with the army commander to protest against the wanton killing of his people, but his pleas were ignored. The commander and his cohorts had no respect for the church because it was questioning the divine right of the national state security to use whatever methods it chose to maintain the status quo.

The murder and persecution increased in El Quiche. The Catholics and some Protestant denominations were now classified as subversives and were subjected to the same liquidation process as the armed guerillas. Despite this, Bishop Gerardi continued to promote peace and justice. His church organised strong communities of people and made all its resources available to nurse the broken bodies and protect the widows and orphans.

Juan Gerardi saw nothing radical in these actions. He was only carrying out his simple pastoral ministry.

Caritas set up a special fund, not for political action, but to provide food and medicine for the victims of this ruthless onslaught.

'Maybe some of those receiving our assistance were guerillas. But when somebody is poor and injured you do not ask for identification,' explained the bishop.

The persecution intensified daily. Then a military death squad assassinated one of Gerardi's priests. The church struggled on, binding up the bodies of the savaged Indians and crying to heaven for an end to this tyranny. A second priest was slaughtered. Still the church refused to cower to this devilish system.

They came again and murdered a third priest. Death warrants were issued for another four priests. God knows how many Indian laymen and women perished during this wave of madness. Further attempts to confront the authorities proved fruitless.

The assault on El Quiche's poor and its church was not restricted to the guns of the armed forces. Right wing groups had entree to the state-controlled radio and they shouted their threats over the airwaves. The radio messages were no more subtle than the death warrants: 'The Catholic Church — get out of El Quiche'.

The division, the fear, the indifference in Guatemala rendered all support for the beleaguered province useless. Dialogue or protest were no longer possible. What should Juan Gerardi do in the face of an all-out massacre of his church? He called together his priests, nuns and leaders of his laity. He was not prepared to adopt the stance of the left and advocate the use of violence. Nor was he willing to watch the wholesale sacrifice of his priests and lay leaders.

After long consultations he made his agonising decision. And we will never know the pain and anguish the bishop went through. After six months of bloodshed and a courageous stand against the powers of hell, his church was finally crucified.

The Bishop of El Quiche announced the closure of his diocese.

A brutal war had been waged against it. In announcing closure of a Catholic diocese in a Catholic country, he probably hoped to awaken the world to this morbid situation.

But the world slept on. Gerardi became a hunted man. During his last weeks in El Quiche, Gerardi was constantly moving from place to place.

'In the end the priests made it clear that it was impossible to continue their ministry. They were scared,' Monsignor Gerardi told me.

The bishop arranged for about 40 priests and nuns to leave

the diocese. Five priests volunteered to stay and minister to their people. The last of the 40 to leave were 20 nuns, who remained to wind up the schools and the administration of the church.

The Diocese of El Quiche was officially sacked on July 20, 1980.

The bishop went to Rome to seek counsel. On his return to Guatemala he was refused entry to his homeland. For the next three years the bishop was exiled to Costa Rica. In spite of this action there was little international protest.

Back in El Quiche, the gates of hell did not close around the little Indian church. New disciples were raised up and the Word of Christ was still proclaimed to the tortured people. It was no longer possible for the clergy to operate; however, a lay church remained. It could not be driven out. It could not be crushed.

Monsignor Gerardi is now back in Guatemala. He cannot return to El Quiche. It remains a military province. He has been told that the right would like to kill him because he's a revolutionary. The left also want to murder him because it says the bishop is a counter-revolutionary.

I sat watching and listening to this man. It was very obvious that he had emerged from the events in El Quiche physically and mentally scarred.

His diocese remains a bulldozed human quagmire. Those of his flock who survived the holocaust are scattered as refugees or caged in a military zoo on the lands they once called home.

He has managed to return to Guatemala but remains in exile from El Quiche.

By world standards his career ended in chaos and his actions have reduced him to an old and broken man. Some might claim cynically that Monsignor Gerardi politicised his community and chose to lead it along the road to destruction. Regardless how one reflects on the tragedy of El Quiche one must acknowledge that Monsignor Juan Gerardi was first and foremost a servant of the God he called Father. It was this relationship that led him to the Indian province and to a total commitment to the people of that place. Therefore failure or success of El Quiche can only be judged by God's standards — not by man's.

Recently I met Monsignor Gerardi again. He is now Auxiliary Bishop of Guatemala City.

I asked him whether, on reflection, he regretted making that decision.

No, was his reply. The position was impossible. If he had stayed many more people would have died.

There are powerful parallels between the dying Christ on Calvary and the bruised and broken church in El Quiche.

As Christ rose from the dead and led his people to salvation, so too will the church of El Quiche rise from the ashes of the villages and the blood of the martyrs to continue its struggle for liberation, peace and justice.

The Father, whose will will be done on earth as in heaven, sent his Son to be the saviour of mankind. The Son was taken, tortured, stripped naked and nailed to a cross.

They offered him wine mixed with myrrh but he refused it, then they crucified him.

The passersby jeered at him. They shook their heads and said: '*Ah. So you would destroy the temple and rebuild it in three days. Then save yourself, come down from the cross*'.

The chief priests and scribes mocked him among themselves in the same way.

Somebody ran and, soaking a sponge in vinegar and putting it on a reed, gave it to him to drink.
— **Mark 15.**

And they seized four of the Christian community and strung them up on the wall of the parish church.

And the captors jeered at the four on the wall, mocking them.

One of the soldiers called to the four hanging on the wall: '*Do you want some water, or a tortilla?*'.
— **A true incident in Guatemala.**

Jovita and Gonzales de Vela and their three children, plus a little friend from the community.

CHAPTER XIII

Two Faces of Faith

Brother Pedro of Guatemala is no run-of-the-mill village patron saint.

Throughout the traditional Catholic world, villagers have adopted their own patron saints. Some have deep Christian significance, others are shrouded in superstition and many are remembered only because their feast day means fiesta, a time of secular celebration, where drinking, eating and dancing become the indispensable form of ritual.

But Brother Pedro is no mere excuse for fiesta. He is a sign that there is a Saviour who loves and defends the poor and powerless. His name is honoured daily, not in the back street bars but in the silence of a church. He has become a symbol for the exploited and abused Indians of Guatemala.

Five hundred years ago this Christian travelled from the Caribbean to share the good news about his God. That commission meant fighting for justice. Single-handed, and without resources, this Bethlemite religious teacher became a servant of the Quechua Indians around the city of Antigua, the former capital of Guatemala.

This was the period when the mighty conquerors were suppressing the last ounce of resistance from the Indian population. Most of the clergy closely identified with the Spanish colonial administration and busied themselves with converting and baptising the savages into God's own European religion.

Few clergymen had any time or inclination to oppose the destruction of a precious Indian culture that was happening

111

before their eyes, and many appeared to accept the brutal killing and persecution of the indigenous people as an allowable method of suppressing opposition to the administration.

Dressed in his shabby brown hessian habit, Brother Pedro dedicated his life to the marginalised. He took care of the sick, and like so many of his modern day Christian brothers and sisters in this region, he ran into conflict with the authorities.

No wonder, therefore, that today thousands of Indians crowd into the huge San Francisco Church, Antigua, to pray to this man. Pedro was like them: poor, rejected and victimised.

Pedro requested that his body be buried in the Franciscan church. His tomb and shrine have withstood a number of earthquakes which have flattened sections of that church.

I watched as Guatemalans came into San Francisco and knocked three times on the door of his tomb, praying and leaving their petitions.

And their prayers were obviously being heard. Hundreds of notes of thanks for petitions granted covered the huge wall near his tomb. Thousands of requests have been answered over the centuries. When the wall is covered, the Franciscan priests remove them, to make room for more to appear.

Many times I have wound my way along the cobblestone streets of Antigua, past the old archways marking the 14 stations of the Cross around the perimeter of San Francisco, and into this church.

To love the poor is to enjoy their company; to share their dreams; witness their process of liberation and be with them in prayer and worship. San Francisco was once an opulent structure, a symbol of beauty but also of the power that seemed to flow from God to his European disciples.

Today the old church, partly in ruins and somewhat dilapidated, has attained new beauty and symbolism. It is the people's church.

Christians claiming more sophisticated understanding of their faith might call this practice of knocking on a dead man's tomb and the lighting of candles before his statue religious superstition. Many of the tourists who flock into the church photograph the ruins and chuckle at the superstition. But they do not have the time to sit and experience the faith of the people around them. They do not realise that San Francisco is not just another piece of antiquity. Here is where the poor and the oppressed come to pay respects to a true follower of Christ.

Pedro did not come to exploit or even convert with a sword. He came to show the face of Christ through love and justice. And when the poor gather around the altar rails they are not reflecting on the little Bethlemite, but on the one who sent Pedro, the one they trust as their liberator.

How easy I found it to fall on my knees and join in this conversation. Words came easily and I became aware of so much around me. There were no distractions; only me, God and those people He loves so much.

Guatemala has been described as the most beautiful place in Latin America. Maybe what makes this nation so memorable are the Mayan Indians. Miraculously, they have survived the Spanish conquest and the structural violence of post-independence military and oligarchic rule.

In rural districts, the Mayan still attempts to survive with the culture and the freedom that was his before the arrival of the Spanish Conquistador, Don Pedro de Alvarado.

Near the centre of Guatemala City, stands a huge stone statue of Tecun Uman. He was the chief of the Quiche Indian tribe (southern Mayan). Tecun was slaughtered by the Conquistador's soldiers, while trying to preserve his people's freedom and dignity.

Not far from the statue is an old bull-fighting ring, Plaza de Toros. The bulls have long gone. However, the crowds are still present. They no longer gleefully call for blood but meekly accept food, medical supplies and call for the freedom to live with the same dignity that Tecun Uman died to preserve.

The old bull ring holds special significance for me. It was there that I was made to think: how would I react if suddenly I lost all my security and all material possessions?

Plaza de Toros evolved after the 1976 earthquake that destroyed so much of the nation. Many of the people sheltering there came from middle-class Latin society.

I met the de Velas: Jovita, her husband Gonzales and the

children Eduardo, Gerardo and Ingrid.

'Our house was modest, but comfortable,' said Jovita.

Before the earthquake, life had been difficult, but hygiene, education, privacy and a reasonable quality of life had been taken for granted by that family.

Then the shuddering Guatemalan landscape changed. Whole areas were razed. The de Velas lost their house, their employment and most of their possessions.

In the space of one day, they had fallen through the fragile layer that separated the lower-middle class from the destitute.

Home was now a single-roomed substandard shack, constructed from discarded iron and timber. It stood in a jungle of squalor.

How did a mother and father cope with that traumatic regression? More than the lack of running water, sanitation and a depressed atmosphere, was the realisation that one was no longer considered an individual human being, but a piece of living rubble that had congregated illegally, and could be shovelled up at any time of day or night. Add to this the knowledge that one's children were no longer free to be children but were confined to a dismal prison; and the fear that you were surrounded by conflict where people had been thrown together, an environment where only the fittest survived.

My faithful World Vision colleague, Dina, had taken me to meet the de Velas. The plan was to visit a number of families in the settlement who were being assisted by the agency.

However, the day passed and I didn't get beyond the de Velas' house.

Jovita could still smile. She wanted to share the transformation that her family lifestyle had suffered. She talked about her fears and the one fortress that she still had, the love of God.

The earthquake had brought ruin to the de Velas. One bed, and an old table — which now served as a playground for the children, a meal table for the family and a workbench for her husband — were all that were salvageable.

The little money they had was used to buy the scrap iron and wood to build the shack. Gonzales and Jovita used the bed, and the children slept on the floor.

In those alleyways of fear, the squatters had not built any form of community. The police constantly hounded the people. The muddy narrow tracks zig-zagging their way through Plaza de Toros were run-offs for the inadequate sanitation system.

Jovita feared those tracks, both the disease that lurked in their every crevice and the confrontation that the confinement bred.

The four corrugated iron walls were her protection. They, too, had become the holding yard for her children. She feared her neighbours and admitted that she refrained from meeting with them and made no attempt to form a community.

The family existed literally on a shoestring. Gonzales had managed to scrape together enough money to set himself up in a small business. He used shoestring to form designs and figures, then inlaid it with crushed, coloured marble. He was able to sell them at the market in Guatemala City.

That tin shanty could hardly be called a house, but there was no doubt in my mind that it was a home.

'We survive here because we are a united family. My husband and I constantly encourage each other,' said Jovita.

Her fortress of hope is Jesus Christ, in whom the family steadfastly believe. The circumstances that have dramatically changed their lives have not injured their relationship with Christ.

A short time after my visit, the people of Plaza de Toros received their marching orders. The government wanted the land cleared.

Some of the families had begun to co-operate together and they refused to leave until the government granted them land to set up a new community.

The military regime promised them Paradise, a new housing estate, on the distant outskirts of the capital.

The soldiers came into Plaza de Toros, breaking down the shanties and loading the scrap onto trucks. More tension and uncertainty for the poor.

Jovita explained to me later that the old bull ring was unsatisfactory, but she had managed to establish a home and the family had come to accept that squatter existence.

Without having a say in their future, the de Velas and hundreds like them were scooped up onto army trucks with the iron sheets and other goods and chattels.

'I was very nervous. The soldiers divided us up. I suffered a nervous breakdown as a result. As we travelled, it poured rain. We were off-loaded into the wet. We were soaked. It reminded me of the time of the earthquake. There was nothing for us. The sky was our roof,' Jovita explained to me during my second visit.

They were dumped like junk into the mud. In a severe state of nervous tension, Jovita became very sick. She rested in a makeshift bed.

'I felt very proud of my husband,' continued Jovita. 'In the rain he put up a house for us in one day.'

The government called the hilly outcrop Paradise.

Instead of muddy tracks, awash with septic water, there were neat concrete paths. A sanitation system had been installed instead of the disease-ridden holes in the ground that the people had used in the bull ring.

But it wasn't long before the people abruptly discovered that Paradise, at least in Guatemala City, was not as the government had promised.

They were many kilometres from the city centre. The bus was too expensive, so many people were unable to reach their places of employment. They were no longer registered as squatters. Instead, the Paradise people discovered that they had to meet water rates, and bank loans to cover the cost of their land, on which they had re-assembled their shanties.

Not-so-subtle pressure had been applied to the people to meet the loans. Now they were motivated to come together as a community. Their very survival was at stake.

Trust was building between these people, who had started off as a cluster of strangers at the old bull ring.

They formed a community committee to discuss the unfair pressures that were being applied. They were unhappy about the lack of transport and schools. When resettlement had been suggested at the Plaza de Toros, officials had not mentioned bank loans.

Then early one morning unidentified men arrived. They rushed from their car to a particular shanty. They knew their man. He was Luis Godoy, the president of the newly-formed community committee. Luis was dragged into the car which quickly sped off. Those who saw the incident wondered if they would ever see their community leader again. Next morning his battered body was found dumped on the doorstep of the community centre.

The people had found the courage to come together and discuss their problems and their rights. But the murder of Luis Godoy struck fear into the hearts of the residents of Paradise. They could not find anybody to take office as community president. Who could be expected to accept a job that meant certain death?

So the committee was disbanded. The people went back behind their shanty walls and were silent.

Since arriving at Paradise, the de Vela family business had gone bust. During the military resettlement to Paradise, all Gonzales' marble and glass were destroyed.

'They dropped our goods off the trucks and broke everything. We were left with nothing. My husband will never recover enough to replace the material that was smashed.'

Gonzales had become a motor mechanic and had moved away to find work. Jovita and the children were left behind.

'The income my husband now gets is $45 a fortnight (the Guatemalan currency was then on par with the US dollar). It is too small. There is hardly enough to buy food', said Jovita.

Jovita was like everybody else — she owed a large amount in back rent.

'I have never owed money like this before. I am worried. Sometimes it is hard to get money together. I have to cut back on food.'

Though feeling desperate, and looking tired and drawn, Jovita had not lost sight of her fortress.

'I believe a miracle will come. I am grateful to God to be alive and living here. He is one who can make miracles.'

Nevertheless, Jovita was extremely disconsolate. The resoluteness that the de Velas had shown at the Plaza de Toros, to

117

face the situation and build a better life, was gone. Jovita cried as she referred to the bank loans and the pressure that was being applied to meet the payments.

The despondency expressed by the de Velas was echoed by others at Paradise.

Even the World Vision project manager, a member of the community, who acted as a link between the people and the agency, also displayed his fear about the future. He spoke in terms of leaving, because the community was claiming that he had let them down. As the community fell deeper into debt and depression, they lost confidence in everybody, including the agency that had been a traditional base of support.

There had been hesitation by the Plaza de Toros people to agree to the resettlement program, but promises had been made, not only by the government but by some welfare groups whom the community trusted.

World Vision was in a dilemma too. It was doing what it could to bolster the deficient school system. It was funding some community self-help programs, but alongside the bank loans and the mounting unemployment, it was no match.

I attempted to encourage Jovita and the project manager to organise the people again into an active community, who could confront the injustices together. As individuals, they were on the edge of despair.

Back in Australia I kept in touch with World Vision Guatemala about the situation in Paradise.

In 1984, I returned and made my third visit to Jovita and her neighbours. I had been warned that I would be met by a different de Vela family. The people were more disillusioned with what appeared to them to be an insurmountable problem.

So I was prepared to be confronted by a disenchanted Jovita. The old galvanised gate that led to her humble house swung open and there was Jovita. I expected the worst.

The first thing I saw was the old smile that I remembered so distinctly at Plaza de Toros. Then I felt her arms around me. Not a word spoken but she was indicating what this visit meant to her. There had been so many do-gooders; so many promises; so much said but immediately forgotten. Yet here was the Australian back again, a third time. He must care; he has not forgotten.

A Jesuit priest, in the slums of Mexico, once explained that communities who have been oppressed and rejected over a number of generations start to believe that they are no good, something less than human. Actions, not words, begin to build new trust that develops into confidence. The Mexican Jesuits did it by leaving their seminary and going out and slumming it with the people. World Vision, in a small way, had done it by bringing me back to Paradise.

Jovita did not want to see the hand-out man with his bags of money, but desperately wanted to feel that somebody cared enough to come and talk with her. Then Jovita took my hand and led me into her home and called to the children. Through the interpreter she told me that Gonzales was home again. He had been laid off as a mechanic because the government had cancelled a contract with his employers. He had managed to scrape up some money and had bought new shoestring and marble.

Little Ingrid, the youngest of the family, jumped onto my knee. On her finger she proudly displayed a small green and yellow bird, a present from her father.

Gonzales was making between six and eight hangings a day from his marble and shoestrings.

'Now Gonzales is selling them himself. There is no middle man. Now that he is working on his own, the children are better fed.'

I mentioned the rent.

'We are still behind. At least I have my children in school,' Jovita said.

But there was still no better community spirit at Paradise.

'I have a problem, because I do not have friends here. I do not like to get involved with other people. I live in my house with my children. That way I do not have more problems. Maybe the problem is that I do not get involved,' admitted Jovita.

However, she was not alone, confirmed the project manager.

'There are many difficulties in this barrio. Nobody wants

to organise a community and find more,' said the project manager.

My visit to Paradise was very beneficial. During that third trip to Guatemala, I had experienced so many negative things. Many had given up the struggle to free themselves from the iron fist of the military. The oppressive system had successfully sown the seeds of fear and disunity in the church and society at large.

Finally, I thought that I was going to lose the relationship that I had established at Paradise.

But Jovita and some of the people there were not prepared to reject a friend. Maybe I had offered some encouragement. Certainly Jovita had given plenty to me. It seemed we both needed each other.

The poor in their misery are not the only ones who sometimes feel as though the forces of evil are too overpowering. The aid workers and the church leaders on the front line also suffer during these periods when they think that everything around them is going to blow up in their faces. Then something happens. The God of the poor, who appears to be sometimes lost in the turmoil, will suddenly stand out in the crowd and everything seems different. His presence gives you new confidence to face the next segment of the journey.

At home I have often reflected on my friends at Paradise, feeling helpless to do anything. In my confused thinking I have wondered why Christ appears to have left that place. Recently I received a letter from Jovita. She told me that she was now actively involved in a church. She and her children were escaping from their galvanised jail to camps and other church functions. She and Gonzales were finding new strength together in their marriage and the people of the community had come together to fight the issue of water. Somebody was trying to overcharge them and the people had had enough.

I wish I had the faith of the Indians who knock on the door of Brother Pedro's tomb and kneel before the high altar in the church of San Francisco and have long conversations with Christ. I wish I had the courage to defend the marginalised, despite the cost, like Brother Pedro. And if my world was to collapse around me, I pray that I would have the same spirit as Jovita, who picks herself up and believes a miracle will come. Jovita, who is grateful to God just to be alive.

Jesus is a human face of God's love for us. Born to Mary and Joseph, he has become part of our human race. He, too, was hungry and in need of friendship. He, too, was besieged by all kinds of human problems. He experienced loneliness and betrayal, rejection and harassment. He had doubts, fears and stage fright. In the last few days of his life he suffered immense pain, collapsed on the streets under the heavy yoke of the cross and asked for water as he hung dying on that cross. The face of the crucified Christ is a human face revealing to us God's intervention in human salvation.

That face is all around us today. It is the face of a tribal chieftain who fears that ancestral land will be lost. It is the face of a peasant's wife who fears her newly-born baby will not live beyond a few months. It is the face of a construction worker who is not sure where his next job will be. It is the face of all those whose last flickering hope is that God will not abandon them.

— Karl Gaspar
Philippines.

A small boy kneels in prayer at the tomb of Oscar Romero. The tomb is in a side chapel at the Metropolitan Cathedral.

CONCLUSION

As the perennial tyranny in Latin America erupted in bloody genocide during the 1970s, some people asked: Where did the church go wrong?

Why wasn't the church about its traditional business of evangelising the pagans, comforting the poor and collaborating with the rich elite to introduce reform? Latin America would seem to be the ideal region of the world for the church to play its traditional role of reconciler and pacifier.

If the issue that has brought turmoil to this region was the rise of revolutionary Marxism, why then is the *church* being persecuted? It would seem that the powerful fear change and in resisting it, have run amok. The church, in affirming its role as defender of the human rights of people, has been pressed into supporting the proponents of change, the reformers.

Vatican II produced the vision — Medellin activated the change in the local Latin Christian communities. For centuries, the church collaborated with the elite, which resulted in much of the church being seen as appeasers rather than reformers.

Honest reflection on the reality in which the church lives has demonstrated the need to evangelise, not primarily the pagans, but the Christians who by their power, greed or silence, show themselves to be godless. And those within the labour and people's movements who were coming together and organising revolutionary change, were not, in the main, pagans but frustrated Christians who felt utterly betrayed by God's representatives.

So Medellin became the benchmark for the Latin church. It provided more than options — it rediscovered authenticity. Its proclamation of 'a preferential option for the poor' was a dramatic reminder to its people that Christ, in Matthew's last judgement, was not the negotiator and bargainer for the hungry and oppressed but had *become* the hungry and the oppressed. The church would stand or fall on this. Already some of the poor were dividing the sheep from the goats.

Therefore, if the people of God had rediscovered authenticity there was no need to borrow inferior ideologies, however noble they might be.

When the national armies were let loose in their countries, they had one goal in mind — to stop the agents of change, both those who had finally chosen to match violence against violence and those who preferred to espouse the Gospel in the face of violence. Christianity and Marxism both represented reform. However, one was easier to dispel. The armed revolutionary forces could be branded Communists, who would not only threaten the powerbrokers in Latin America, but the United States and the rest of the free world as well.

The more dangerous agents of change were the poor in their communities who put their hope for the future in Jesus Christ. How could the Latin oligarchs and militaries allow this group to survive? Christianity is at the heart of the Latin culture. It is the soul of Latin existence. Therefore, the authentic Gospel had to be quickly eradicated and replaced by the old traditional and compromising church. But no longer was the responsibility of the church in the hands of a few bishops. Clergy, religious and laity were all sharing the ministry together and learning from one another.

Here was the church of the incarnated God, confronting the tyrants and demanding justice for its people.

No wonder Salvadoran and Jesuit Rutilio Grande wrote: 'I'm quite aware that very soon the Bible and the Gospel won't be allowed to cross our borders. We'll get only the bindings because all the pages are subversive.

'It is dangerous to be a Christian in our world.'

No wonder the military-backed death squads earmarked the Base Christian Communities and the progressive clergy as their prime targets.

From this authentic church came the inspiration, not from glossy heroes but genuine grass-roots saints.

People like Father Rutilio Grande, who thought the priesthood was reaching out for perfection, his understanding of perfection. His sainthood developed when he realised his sinfulness and went out in faith and worked within his limitations.

Grande never reached the perfection he once chased but reached people he never dreamed he could.

The life of this Salvadoran Jesuit affords us a glimpse of the struggle by the poor, for liberation via a third way. There is so much weakness and fragility in this man's story. The long years of uncertainty and passiveness were the struggle he fought to find his vocation. There was never much doubt that Grande ever wanted to be anything but a priest. When he stumbled and doubted it was because he was deciding what type of priest he should be. Like the people he served, Grande was frightened and unsure. However, when he was prepared to understand the mind of Christ and see the opportunities available to him, he became a committed disciple to the oppressed. Boldly, he condemned the neo-feudal structure that enslaved most of the Salvadoran nation. Boldly, he attempted to escalate the church's journey with the poor.

'We must break open a breach in our Wailing Wall in order to thrust into life the drama of faith as a story of liberation ... From sterile immobility, which gives us a false sense of security, let us leap out of security, let us leap out and run the risk and the adventure of living a life of fidelity, in movement, in existential and dramatic tension! In crisis!', said Rutilio.

But like the military, many church authorities moved to silence the priest. He was sacked as professor of pastoral theology and director of social action at the national diocesan seminary, San Jose de la Montana, San Salvador.

But neither government nor traditional church could accuse Rutilio Grande of aligning himself with the armed liberation forces. The Jesuit had no reason to link himself to government or guerilla. His obligation was only to a salvation through which communities plotted their own course — a salvation that was based on free will and not force. A salvation that excluded no one — rich, poor, soldier or guerilla.

He was a dangerous man, an unacceptable liberator to any institution committed to a worldly doctrine. So the state had him murdered — the first time Salvador had ordered the execution of a member of the clergy.

This was an important chapter in the transfiguration of the church and the poor.

Oh how I wish I had met Rutilio.

The church, the people of God in their Base Christian Communities, have not been destroyed in spite of a long period of genocide. I believe they represent the indestructible liberation of the poor.

Recently one Christian community celebrated the passion of Jesus Christ and remembered members of its own community — 401 assassinated in seven years. In El Salvador between 1980 and 1982 many members of these communities were killed or disappeared. Since 1983, little by little they have grown again.

'To me' says Jesuit theologian Jon Sobrino, 'they are the leaven of the whole church. Having everything against them, the army, the security forces, the oligarchy, the US Embassy, and even some bishops, they have not disappeared.

'Their faith is real and deeply rooted in this country.

'Martyrdom in 1980 to 1982 is why they declined and martyrdom is why since that time they are active and growing.'

Father Jon Sobrino says that our faith is at stake unless Christians are 'prepared to accompany the poor into conflict zones, not to become guerillas, but just to be there, listening, risking all to be there'.

I have not yet had the courage to accompany them into conflict zones.

I pray that one day I will.